Communicating Corporate
Social Responsibility

Communicating Corporate Social Responsibility

The Trust Factor

Kristie Byrum

LEXINGTON BOOKS
Lanham • Boulder • New York • London

Published by Lexington Books
An imprint of The Rowman & Littlefield Publishing Group, Inc.

4501 Forbes Boulevard, Suite 200, Lanham, Maryland 20706
www.rowman.com

86-90 Paul Street, London EC2A 4NE, United Kingdom

Copyright © 2023 by The Rowman & Littlefield Publishing Group, Inc.

All rights reserved. No part of this book may be reproduced in any form or by any electronic or mechanical means, including information storage and retrieval systems, without written permission from the publisher, except by a reviewer who may quote passages in a review.

British Library Cataloguing in Publication Information Available

Library of Congress Cataloging-in-Publication Data

Names: Byrum, Kristie, author.
Title: Communicating corporate social responsibility : the trust factor / Kristie Byrum.
Description: Lanham : Lexington Books, [2023] | Includes bibliographical references and index. | Summary: "Communicating Corporate Social Responsibility: The Trust Factor explores theoretical frameworks and practical applications for creating trust between an organization and key stakeholders. Scholars of communication, public relations, and leadership will find this book of particular interest"—Provided by publisher.
Identifiers: LCCN 2022046766 (print) | LCCN 2022046767 (ebook) | ISBN 9781793646484 (cloth ; alk. paper) | ISBN 9781793646507 (pbk. : alk. paper) | ISBN 9781793646491 (epub)
Subjects: LCSH: Social responsibility of business. | Communication.
Classification: LCC HD60 .B95 2023 (print) | LCC HD60 (ebook) | DDC 658.4/08—dc23/eng/20221125
LC record available at https://lccn.loc.gov/2022046766
LC ebook record available at https://lccn.loc.gov/2022046767

∞™ The paper used in this publication meets the minimum requirements of American National Standard for Information Sciences—Permanence of Paper for Printed Library Materials, ANSI/NISO Z39.48-1992.

In memory of Reed Bolton Byrum, Sr., APR, Fellow PRSA

and

For my children, Bradley, Caroline and James

Contents

Preface	ix
Introduction	1
Chapter 1: The Corporate Social Responsibility/Corporate Reputation Connection	5
Chapter 2: Overcoming Skepticism with the Trust Factor: A Corporate Social Responsibility Communication Process Model	23
Chapter 3: A Credible Source to Carry the Corporate Social Responsibility Message	33
Chapter 4: Creating and Sharing Credible CSR Information	45
Chapter 5: Social Media Engagement in a CSR Program	57
Chapter 6: Promoting Purchase Intention through Corporate Social Responsibility Communication	69
Chapter 7: Measuring Corporate Social Responsibility Programs	85
Chapter 8: The Future of CSR Communication	99
Bibliography	105
Index	119
About the Author	123

Preface

This text arrives at a time when the world faces a global pandemic brought about by Covid-19. With the dynamics of public health and safety, strained supply chains, and workers telecommuting from remote environments, corporations face a business environment drastically transformed by a global pandemic. With these vast changes in the working environment, corporations have attempted to nimbly adapt to new circumstances, pivoting corporate social responsibility activities to more specifically address the particular needs of employees and all stakeholders. Yet with the imperative to think and act strategically and usefully to address the Covid-19 pandemic, many companies have continued existing CSR programs that are strategic and core to the business. Further, management teams have dealt with the changing circumstances yet simultaneously have gone back to basics, determining the appropriate CSR effort, the appropriate spokesperson, and the appropriate channels for communication. Stakeholders demand a greater level of accountability for the corporation and today businesses are finding ways to address varying concerns while coping with the global pandemic. This text sets forth a corporate social responsibility communication process model with five distinct phases. You will find information about how various businesses have faced pandemic-related corporate social responsibility efforts by looking at companies in technology, food, housing, and transportation. With the vital need to accurately communicate to multiple stakeholders across the miles, at a time when employees and others may face dire personal situations from the global pandemic, this text addresses the role of the trusted source in carrying the message to the marketplace. With the proliferation of online social media environments, consumers were left scrambling to find accurate information. To focus on authentic and accurate communication, companies deployed a full array of media options including paid, earned, shared, and owned media channels to convey messages and get feedback from individuals inside and outside of the corporation. By successfully employing dialogic principles, companies now found themselves communicating with stakeholders in a meaningful way, fueling the viral spread of information and creating feedback loops. The imperative to remain profitable and provide for others remains vital for the corporation and this text reveals evidence regarding how corporate social responsibility programs can stimulate the purchase of goods and services by endearing the corporation through trust and authentic branding through corporate social responsibility. By establishing the right program and deploying the effort with the right message and the appropriate spokesperson, the corporation can harvest vast benefits. This text also reveals how companies can measure the effectiveness of the CSR effort and perform modifications as necessary. While the Covid-19 pandemic brought the world to a state of emergency and corresponding confusion as businesses tackled new business models and modes of operation, the corporate social responsibility environment also evolved, showing the interconnectedness between corporations and various stakeholders.

Introduction

This text addresses the presence of corporate social responsibility communication in our society. While companies grapple to address the interconnectedness between corporate functions and the society at large, the role of the corporate communicator comes into focus. A corporate social responsibility campaign without communication will fall flat and fail to gain the desired accomplishments that management teams seek to gain. This book examines both research and practical implications for the professional corporate social responsibility communicator.

Chapter 1, "The Corporate Social Responsibility/Corporate Reputation Connection," acquaints the reader with the connection between corporate social responsibility programs, corporate reputation, and brand management. Through an exploration of the corporate-stakeholder bond, the reader is able to interpret the business impact of irresponsible branding and more fully appreciate the role of the public relations professional. The public relations professional is uniquely positioned to carry the CSR message, as evidenced by the fact the professional has an understanding of various stakeholders. We observe a shift from a sender-receiver model of communication to a dialogic one with a sensitivity to determining the appropriate source for the communication and choosing the right medium to communicate, businesses can gain greater traction in the corporate social responsibility initiatives. This chapter reveals to readers corporate strategies used to communicate with various stakeholders during the global pandemic. You will learn about corporate programs at Intel, Microsoft, Campbell's Soup, General Mills, and others as companies coped with the pandemic. You will also learn about corporate social responsibility efforts during other emergency situations such as Airbnb's efforts to provide housing for Afghanistan refugees. The chapter explains how management teams adapted to changing circumstances yet remained focused on building communities and collaborating with stakeholders.

Chapter 2, "Overcoming Skepticism with the Trust Factor: A Corporate Social Responsibility Communication Process Model," addresses sound techniques for using dialogic communication to communicate with key stakeholders. While skepticism can occur, specific approaches may be explored to reduce and erase feelings of doubt in exchange for a richer, authentic relationship with key stakeholders. Living in the modern world, businesses today exert the brand through corporate social responsibility programs and can successfully bind stakeholders to the organization in both the short term and long term. With this in mind, this text proposes a new corporate social responsibility communication process model. The model contains five distinct phases: Phase 1, strategic CSR investigation and program creation; Phase 2, communications planning that considers elements including the source, media format, and sentiments expressed via social media; Phase 3, communication deployment; Phase 4, co-creation with the audience; and Phase 5, communication measurement. As the reader explores the role of corporate social responsibility in reaching various stakeholders and building the corporate reputation, the role of key influencers and the co-creation of media content becomes apparent.

Chapter 3, "A Credible Source to Carry the Corporate Social Responsibility Message," assesses the use of various sources. When considering "who" carries the message, chapter 3 explores how various sources are used to carry the corporate social responsibility message. With the evolution in dialogic communication, the chapter explores the use of person-to-person communication, allowing the reader to better understand the distinct roles of the consumer and the public relations professional. The chapter uncovers the enhanced role of the information receiver as they attribute information to the sender and formulate their own perspectives on the legitimacy of the corporate social responsibility program. The chapter further includes ten tips for creating dialogues, giving practitioners key insights on how to relate to and motivate consumers to engage in a corporate social responsibility program.

Chapter 4, "Creating and Sharing Credible CSR Information," provides readers with key insights on appropriate channel selection and message creation for a corporate social responsibility campaign. With the appropriate spokesperson selected, public relations professionals can proceed with determining the appropriate channels for communication and relevant messages that will resonate with stakeholders. Chapter 4 explores various dimensions of media credibility and explains how accurate, credible information can advance the corporate social responsibility program. The text provides the reader with tips for communicating online about CSR and provides five key approaches for CSR communication that leads to consumer engagement and participation. This chapter provides readers with theoretical foundations and practical applications of how to determine the appropriate communication mix. With a discussion of paid, earned, shared, and owned media, the chapter gives the reader key insights on how practitioners deploy an effective corporate social responsibility communication program.

Chapter 5, "Social Media Engagement in a CSR Program," addresses social media engagement in a corporate social responsibility program. The chapter examines the interaction between source credibility and social media viral spread. With the ubiquity of social media, we observe the evolution of media relations and note how various media formats fuel online word of mouth. The chapter further examines the use of dialogic principles in social media and how media consumers become content producers in corporate social responsibility programs. The chapter further explains the impact of technology and web-enabled social media channels on corporate social responsibility programs.

Chapter 6, "Promoting Purchase Intention through Corporate Social Responsibility Communication," examines how corporate social responsibility communication can help drive product sales and interaction with a corporation. With higher levels of consumer engagement, the company may advance stakeholder trust in the program and lead to desired purchasing behaviors. The chapter explores the notion of social status gained through CSR program participation and demonstrates how co-creation of content with multiple stakeholders leads to business results.

Chapter 7, "Measuring Corporate Social Responsibility Programs," gives the reader key insights on how to evaluate the performance of the corporate social responsibility program. The author demonstrates how to implement the Barcelona Principles of Measurement to a CSR campaign and explains proper measurement techniques for key influencers and social media activity. In a discussion of CEO activism, the author further explores how executives lead from the top to convey CSR programs.

Chapter 8, "The Future of CSR Communication," offers insights into the immediate and longer-term outlook for trust-based corporate social responsibility communication programs. Overall, this text provides readers with a contemporary view of corporate social responsibility communication derived from key lessons learned during the global pandemic and maturation of the dialogic era of social media communication.

Chapter 1

The Corporate Social Responsibility/Corporate Reputation Connection

Corporate social responsibility has emerged as more than just a company "giving back" to the local community. Amid an atmosphere of global pandemic brought on by Covid-19 and subsequent variants, management teams have actively exerted creativity and delivered new ways for corporations to cooperate with the publics they serve. With quarantine protocols and legal regulations, contemporary businesses redefined working situations and exhibited a richer level of interaction with employees, customers, and all aspects of the supply chain. While corporate social responsibility has long been a discipline of enlightened companies and management teams, the global pandemic and resulting crises have thrust employers into a more responsible role as they make policies, care for employees, and set the tone for employers nationally. This text explores various aspects of corporate social responsibility communication within the context of building trust. Undertaking CSR programs to bind stakeholders to the organization has long been recognized by scholars in multiple disciplines including management, marketing, and ethics. The role of communication in binding the stakeholder to the organization during a corporate social responsibility program requires careful thought and diligent implementation. Maignan and Ferrell (2004) provide an integrative framework for the reasons why corporations devise CSR programs, dissecting them into socially driven, stakeholder-driven, management-driven, and ethical practices. They assert the CSR may bond the firm and its stakeholders, with communication stimulating interactions both with and between stakeholders. The global pandemic has allowed corporations to take a crystal-clear look at various stakeholders and prioritize their importance and relevance. In analyzing public trust and credibility in various institutions, the Edelman Trust Barometer 2021 found that business has emerged as the most trusted institution, replacing government (Edelman 2021). This stands to reason considering the role of the employer in conveying policies and procedures for Covid safety.

The concepts of philanthropy remain woven into the fabric of literature, religious doctrines, and ethics codes. The meaning of philanthropy has morphed through thousands of years, and today corporations wrestle with the concept of corporate social responsibility (CSR) as a strategic business dimension used to interact with multiple stakeholders. Today, chief executive officers, marketing executives, public relations professionals, and boards of directors contemplate notions of strategic philanthropy, cause marketing, and the "triple bottom line" of people, planets, and profit, all driven by the overarching need to engage with stakeholders. In recent history, businesses have relied on traditional media formats like newspapers and magazines in the wide array of print and broadcast media to convey points about CSR initiatives, but today corporate communicators face a fountainhead of media content fueled by social media.

To enlighten the discussion of CSR communication, it is important to understand the business backdrop for communication that conveys corporate goodwill and citizenship. The ability to transact relies on the seller's ability to convey the value proposition to a prospective buyer and interpret the buyer's acceptance or denial. Persuasion plays a vital role and the ethos of the speaker, the pathos of the appeal, and the logos of the argument vary among each transaction. The seller and buyer either arrive at an agreement in the exchange of the goods and services or retreat from the deal. Commercial communication exchanges have come a long way from ancient bartering to contemporary digital exchanges that fuel transactions twenty-four/seven from buyers and sellers who may never meet in person but merely exchange data to promote a sale. Yet the compelling challenge to articulate value propositions by commanding multimedia channels now at our disposal remains the same. Public relations practitioners and scholars continue to explore aspects of corporate communications by probing the following: Who says what to whom? Who is the most credible and trustworthy individual to carry the corporation's CSR message? What is the best media format to credibly convey information? What is the impact of CSR on purchase intent, the brand, and social media engagement? What is the impact of testimonial sentiment on social media engagement? Corporations today remain perplexed about these dynamics as new channels for message distribution, communications influences, and vehicles for communication alter the influences on the consumer. Questions about what is said, to whom, by whom, and for what purpose continually confound the marketplace and leave public relations practitioners with ongoing dilemmas when planning and implementing corporate social responsibility programs. A frequent leader in corporate social responsibility communication has been the public relations professional.

PUBLIC RELATIONS CONTEXT

While various spokespersons may be called on to carry the corporate social responsibility message, scholars argue that the public relations professional is most advantageously positioned to handle CSR communication. The role of the public relations professional in corporate communications continues to evolve. The public relations professional has at times moved beyond a traditional press agentry role to a more advanced and strategic role as a communicator who shapes and frames communication in dialogic engagement. Various media formats have been used by public relations professionals including news releases, paid advertisements, and social media content to convey corporate information. The public relations professional may devise and deploy a corporate social responsibility campaign to assist with corporate meaning making and sensemaking for society. The arguments below include discussions about the "expert prescriber role" of the professional and the fact that public relations is a profession with an agreed-upon code of ethics. Further, the public relations professional possesses the ability to understand the needs of multiple stakeholders encompassing internal and external publics. Lastly, the public relations professional, operating under the dialogic principles of communication, may build mutually beneficial relationships between an organization and its publics, fully delivering on the contemporary practice of public relations. Scholars cite public relations professionals as experts who have the capacity to perform a strategic role in the planning and implementation of corporate social responsibility campaigns. As expert prescribers counseling the senior management team, public relations professionals are uniquely qualified to undertake the corporate social responsibility program (Freitag, 2005). This is due in part to the ability of public relations professionals to understand, interpret, and advance stakeholder communication, based on the multiple CSR aspects including legal, ethical, environmental, and philanthropic dimensions, as defined by Carroll (1979). As active players in corporate social responsibility, public relations practitioners must foster mutually beneficial relationships with all stakeholders to achieve harmony and prevent a "legitimacy gap" from occurring when a company does not meet society's expectations (Daugherty, 2001). Signitzer and Prexl (2008) identified the competitive advantages of the public relations discipline, pointing to the professional's preferred role as CSR communicator rather than human resources, quality management, or sustainable divisions. The public relations professional has the following attributes that bolster a position in

CSR communication: skills segmenting target audiences, personal knowledge of stakeholders, education and experience, expertise in internal communication, ability to react to conflict with consensus orientation, and a depth of experience in sustainable communications (Signitzer & Prexl, 2008). Yet the perception of the public relations professional remains limited by perceptions of media relations and publicity. White and Park (2010) found that public relations remains closely tied with publicity and media relations, with more than half of the respondents believing that public relations and media relations were synonymous (White & Park, 2010). This gap denotes the schism between the publicity agent model and the expert-prescriber model of public relations.

Other public relations scholars have called for CSR leadership by the public relations professional (Starck & Kruckeberg, 2001). The public relations practitioner should be primarily responsible for fostering and nurturing consumer communities while leveraging positive community benefits and minimizing negative outcomes to individuals, society, and the social environment (Kruckeberg et al., 2006). It is recognized that scholars call for the "expert prescriber" or "public relations professional," rather than a public relations tactician (Dozier, 1995; Freitag, 2005). This distinction defines a demarcation between a strategic communicator and a tactics-based worker devoted to disseminating publicity content. The perception of the public relations professional in a one-dimensional role of publicity agent must be shed to make way for the expanded role of the strategic communicator in corporate social responsibility. CSR has ebbed and flowed for more than a century as management struggled to balance responsibilities to shareholders. Doing so will require informed and unemotional examination of carefully developed policy possibilities, followed by high-order public discourse. Public relations managers are uniquely positioned, experienced, and qualified to guide that effort (Freitag, 2005, p. 40). As the role of the public relations professional is contemplated in the context of corporate social responsibility communication, it is relevant to consider additional factors that endorse the rationale for leadership of the public relations professional in the area of CSR communication.

Corporate Social Responsibility Communication

New technologies and the creation of dialogic communication channels like social networks alter the environment for corporations seeking to engage with stakeholders in a CSR program. Several scholars have applied this theoretical approach of dialogic communication to corporate social responsibility. Clark (2000) points to corporate social responsibility as a manifestation that business and society are interwoven and that business has a responsibility to respond to society needs and pressures. Whether a CSR campaign exists in a formative roll-out stage or is moving to maturity, the communication imperative remains. Another endorsement of strategic communication is presented by Coombs and Holladay (2012), who call for the integration of communication into all phases of the corporate social responsibility process. The pair determine a model for CSR communication that encompasses scanning and monitoring of the environment to determine potential CSR programs, undertaking formative research, creating a program, communicating a CSR initiative that uses a multifaceted communication campaign, and then properly evaluating and providing feedback (Coombs & Holladay, 2012). Today, public relations practitioners continue to explore the most effective media formats and media channels to convey corporate social responsibility information.

Corporations may use CSR activities to enfranchise stakeholders and promote actions that allow the corporation to achieve desired business outcomes. Communication may be effectively utilized to promote collaboration among key stakeholders involved in a CSR campaign. Consumers may assign attributes to the corporation such as self-interest or a profit focus when examining a CSR program. For example, we now observe active co-creation of content among stakeholders in media channels. Sometimes corporations operating in an atmosphere of distrust may use CSR as a tool for co-creation of content, developed in a dialogic manner that promotes trust and enhances the bond between the stakeholder and the corporation. Despite the level of trust or credibility a corporation has with its stakeholders, corporate social responsibility (CSR) remains a relevant and contemporary agenda item for corporations that seek to engage in a meaningful way with the constituents that they serve. Further, with research indicating that corporate social responsibility may have a positive impact on the bottom line and promote many positive dimensions including brand reputation and product trial, scholars and businesses seek richer knowledge about corporate social responsibility and effective means for communicating.

The dialogic dimension of rich communication between an organization and its key publics is fertile area when considering CSR communication. Research in the arena of corporate social responsibility and communication reveals insights about the formation of relationships and dialogues between a corporation and its key publics. Further, public relations practitioners have gained executive roles in the strategic planning of CSR programs and corresponding communication programs. Through the implementation of these activities, the public relations professional actively works to help the corporation form a community and promote co-creation of corporate brands and fuel purchase intention (Byrum, 2017). Ongoing debates persist about the effects of various media formats and sources on believability of CSR messages. Yet amid the global pandemic, corporations turned to internal communication methods, notably corporate-owned media channels including direct email correspondence, mobile messaging, and emergency response technologies to convey accurate information to employees. It is important for us to examine strategies that companies have used to communicate with various stakeholders during the global pandemic. Further, we can identify the relationship between the corporation and key stakeholders in the midst of the global pandemic. As we evaluate the effectiveness of various corporate social responsibility programs devised to help stakeholders cope with the changing circumstances brought about by Covid-19, we learn how stakeholders have adapted to the pandemic circumstances with the help of corporate social responsibility programs. Lastly, through this exploration, we can derive lessons from the innovative approaches that corporations have undertaken that specifically address how the corporation communicated with the stakeholders to derive mutual benefits.

The global pandemic propelled by Covid-19 has brought corporate social responsibility to a new era. As corporations struggled to find their way in a new environment that included supply chain issues, government intervention, and quarantines for employees and customers, management teams across the globe struggled to find answers on how to reduce or alleviate the total business impact while simultaneously helping key stakeholders cope with dire health circumstances. Vulnerable individuals in the global society faced even more uncertainty and fear from basic human needs including food, shelter, and access to proper medical treatment. As governments across the globe instituted new policies for wearing mask, immunizations, and Covid testing, corporations faced the daunting challenge of determining ways to "pivot" that would allow the company to remain in business and allow the employees, customers, vendors, and communities at large to survive the dire circumstances. With an eye on the safety and security of human beings, corporations are best served by utilizing strategic thinking and innovation to deal with the constantly changing circumstances fueled by the global pandemic.

Corporate Actions during Covid-19

In 2021, Intel launched a $50 million Pandemic Response Technology Initiative (PRTI), to determine innovative uses for technology to address Covid-19. The company stated that its goal was to "provide a 360-degree view of the challenges ahead, focusing on how our technologies can enhance healthcare, education and the economic recovery of businesses at multiple levels." With this strategic focus, the company set out to provide short-term relief and longer-term innovation, resulting in 230 projects in collaboration with 170 organizations (Intel, 2022). In January 2020, Microsoft launched the company's AI for Health program designed to utilize data to improve health across the globe. The company quickly found itself in the middle of the global pandemic, and by April fully mobilized the program to focus on the front lines of Covid research (Microsoft, 2022). By funding more than 150 grants, the company has further enabled research for pandemic treatment and diagnostics, basic scientific research and data, and insights into the pandemic (Microsoft, 2022). While it is important to note the Covid-specific corporate social responsibility efforts of these companies, it should also be recognized that these companies did not wander away from existing corporate social responsibility efforts on other core areas.

In a corporate social responsibility report, Campbell's Soup credits itself with enabling food access across the United States during the Covid-19 pandemic by increasing production to help meet demand. Further the company states that it donated over $8 million in cash and in-kind donations to community organizations in the thirty-three Campbell hometowns, as it pursued a corporate social responsibility campaign that focused on issues that were material to the company, have served as a historic strength of the company, and could allow the company to successfully leverage the brand in meaningful ways to have a measurable impact on the community (Campbell, 2022).

General Mills reported that the company provided 17 million meals in 2021 by working with Feeding America, as the company's brands such as Cheerios, Golden Graham's, Betty Crocker, and others addressed the challenge of food insecurity and hunger. These donations came at a time when the General Mills Foundation also reported a $9 million grant program that helped citizens in need. Lastly, the company also reported that employees logged more than 8,000 volunteer hours during the pandemic (General Mills, 2022). Global pharmaceutical company, AbbVie, donated $35 million to support the Covid-relief effort, including a donation to the International Medical Corps to relieve capacity at overburdened hospitals and create mobile field hospitals (AbbVie, 2022). When it comes to transportation, companies were reaching out to key stakeholders with solutions. Lyft provided $4 million in cleaning supplies and protective equipment to drivers and offered healthcare workers rides (Lyft, 2022). Research has found that corporate advocacy leads to relational communication, which in turn strengthens the bond between the organization and the public and engenders support for the organization (Browning et al., 2020).

Corporate Social Responsibility during Emergencies

In 2021, the United States withdrew troops from Afghanistan, leading to a refugee crisis, as citizens sought to leave the war-torn country. Private company Airbnb stepped in to provide relief. In a collaboration with existing nonprofit organizations focused on resettlement such as HIAS, CWS, and Rescue.org, Airbnb boasts that it was committed to providing stays for 20,000 refugees, providing an immediate framework for Airbnb hosts to offer relief for the refugees (Airbnb, 2022). This corporate social responsibility effort is strategically sound and meaningful for multiple stakeholders. While the corporate social responsibility paradigm often focuses on stakeholders outside of the organization and building communities, the global pandemic allowed organizations to take care of their own through creative internal programs. For example, real estate investment company CBRE created the CBRE Employee Resilience Fund with an initial company donation to assist employees struggling with the economic impact of Covid-19, with the program providing more than 16,000 grants (CBRE, 2022).

Scholars who study corporate communication have examined the phenomenon of corporate social responsibility from multiple vantage points and found corporate social responsibility yields various effects for the consumer. Research indicates that positive perceptions of perceived corporate social responsibility influence the consumer's purchase intention behavior and promote corporate donations to corporate-supported nonprofit organizations (Pirsch et al., 2007). Brand benefits and other intangible, or goodwill, value may also result from corporate social responsibility (Murray & Vogel, 1997). Consumer actions that result from consumer exposure to corporate social responsibility may not be tied to a specific product, but assist with advancing the corporate brand (Brown et al., 2007). The corporate quest to grow the bottom line, enhance corporate reputation, and bind stakeholders to the company is now intertwined with corporate social responsibility and the ability to influence stakeholders in the social media sphere. Publicly traded and private companies maintain active corporate social responsibility programs and often utilize social media to carry the message.

It may be asserted that the logical and planned joining of stakeholder dialogue and corporate social responsibility will generate corporate value by prompting specific consumer actions and promoting advantageous beliefs. With social media, co-creation of brands and corporate identity no longer remain solely in the hands of the corporations, but now the stakeholder audience wields a stronger role. Through communication, stakeholders are enabled to participate, engage, and transform the corporate brand. A global pandemic pressing on the infrastructure of corporate brands requires creativity and thoughtfulness for all communication. The stakeholder publics—vendors, employees, shareholders, and others—rise to a more prominent position. Consumers skilled at enduring market circumstances during the global pandemic share information and can collaborate with the company to advance corporate messages. In fact, scholars such as Morsing and Schultz (2006) found new structures for stakeholder involvement to encompass collaboration emerging more than a decade ago, but co-creation has advanced based on market conditions and the advent of new social media technologies that ease co-creation. Instead of imposing corporate norms for CSR initiatives on stakeholders, the invitation to participate and co-construct the corporate CSR message increases the likelihood that these stakeholders and those who identify with them will identify positively with the company (Morsing & Schultz, 2006). So it can be observed that the advent of social media has created an environment whereby co-created brands and negotiated brands emerge as the norm, not the exception. By carrying increased power to create and disseminate corporate information, the focus may now be shifting to the consumer. Though corporations have multiple stakeholders, consumers represent a critical stakeholder relationship.

When faced with the decision to purchase a product as part of a corporate social responsibility program, customers take into consideration many variables: How much does the product cost? Does it resonate with my core values? Is this company authentic in creating this work? At times, customers want to support a company that reflects a higher ideal, something that the consumer can truly rally behind while making an informed purchase. Existing research suggests a company becomes attractive to an individual when that person can identify with the company (Bhattacharya & Sen, 2003). This connection resonates with the elaboration likelihood model of persuasion as audiences "elaborate" on CSR messages as they integrate corporate messages with individual value systems and tend to support or reject a corporate CSR platform. This logic trajectory then extends to corporate social responsibility programs, as companies boost their nonprofit associations, articulate programs, and educate key stakeholders to enhance firm attractiveness. This proactive approach generates a direct influence on corporate social responsibility activities. There is a positive correlation between identity attractiveness and a consumer's positive emotional attitude toward the corporation (Marin & Ruiz, 2007). To expand, it was found that the presence of corporate social responsibility programs can make a company more attractive for consumers by appealing to their social identity. By accentuating values-driven concepts, the corporation enhances the consumer-company bond (Bhattacharya & Sen, 2003). This corporate-to-consumer bond is fragile and companies must seek to avoid "greenwashing" or blatant self-promotion, because such actions can precipitate a negative impact on the corporation's brand, sales, and perception. All of these variables swirl around the corporate social responsibility purchasing decision, giving citizens new environments to deliberate about corporate brands.

After a company decides to conduct a corporate social responsibility program, it is important to choose the correct one and guard against blatant, profit-driven motives. Scholarship has found that CSR initiatives that are a low "fit" with the preferences of the customer base may have a negative impact on consumer beliefs, attitudes, and intentions (Becker-Olsen et al., 2005). Further, "high-fit" programs with a singular profit motive have the same negative impact. Corporate executives facing Covid-19 and the resulting variants, supply chain issues, disenfranchised workers, and confused customers must deliberately choose a corporate social responsibility effort that will resonate with respective audiences to build the brand, rather than lead to further alienation. If selected and executed properly, the positive results abound as corporations advance their brand, promote sales, and solidify corporate trust. In fact, consumers assume a company is skilled at making reliable products when the business has a strong corporate social responsibility program (Kim et al., 2005). As we take a look back at the heritage of CSR, we can note a field that continues to evolve with ubiquity of one-to-one dialogues and key influencers emerging on social media platforms. The company no longer communicates with the stakeholders in an one-way, "authoritarian" way, but rather now engages in a rich, at times unpredictable dialogue with multiple publics.

BEYOND THE SENDER-RECEIVER MODEL TO DIALOGIC COMMUNICATION

The transmission of corporate social responsibility information allows for interpretation by distinct audiences. The role of the audience must also be considered as audience members may perform an active role in creating understanding and interpreting information. Ultimately, the audience may become an active participate in the co-creation of corporate messages. Starck and Kruckeberg (2001) have pointed to the role of the audience in the creation of communities around corporations and products, while Kent and Taylor (2002) consider the role of the audience as an actor in the dialogic communication. Further, movements away from sender-receiver models of communication, as articulated by Hall (1980), pave the way for new concepts of sensemaking and co-creation.

Every corporate social responsibility campaign is undertaken for a specific purpose. These reasons may encompass strategic business decisions that influence the supply chain, product development, or marketing. Further, each collective audience and individual audience member brings a unique perspective to the table that colors the perception of the message. Scholarly literature on corporate social responsibility addresses the audience role by considering stakeholder-driven motives (Basu & Palazzo, 2008) for undertaking a CSR program. Further, these have been categorized into stakeholder information strategies, stakeholder response strategies, and stakeholder involvement strategies (Morsing & Schultz, 2006). With the benefit of various perspectives and values, citizens communicate with their peers and influence them with particular opinions and values. Korschun and Du (2013) have asserted that audience co-creation in corporate social responsibility may lead to immediate outcomes of community participation and formation of corporate social responsibility expectations. As stakeholders attempt to perceive information, they may enhance their level of scrutiny of specific messages and become less susceptible to peripheral cues (Petty & Cacioppo, 1986). Corporations today seeking a magic bullet for communication of corporate social responsibility communication will not find one, as each circumstance presents different variables and each audience engages in a unique way. The corporate social responsibility equation is far more complicated and requires diligent care to various sources and media formats.

Corporate Social Responsibility Information Sources and Media Formats

Corporations deal with issues related to source and format to convey product information and investor relations materials. However, corporate social responsibility information presents a different challenge because it can become an area of distrust and be wrongly perceived by the audience. Misunderstood CSR programs can damage the brand, thus further underscoring the need for appropriate fit and attribution of goodwill instead of blatant commercialism. Communication plays a vital role in this process. This is further reflected as scholars have denoted a shift from a sender-based to a receiver-based model of communication (Springston, 2001). While drowning in data and compelled by the need to understand social, economic, and political communication, individuals will form niche communities to demand and process information.

They assert that through CSR, stakeholders can become brand ambassadors and exert influence through word of mouth and that attribution plays a role in interpreting CSR motives and companies should seek CSR programs that demonstrate a good "fit" with important stakeholders. These researchers indicate that CSR communication via corporate sources may trigger skepticism and that companies should instead strive for unbiased media coverage and utilize social media to disseminate information about a corporate social responsibility program. When examining word of mouth, the use of virtual reality and immersive videos in corporate social responsibility programs seems to advance the relationship between the organization and the public because the videos provide added benefits of interaction (Cheng et al., 2022). With these new media formats the onus resides with the management and communications professionals to discern the appropriate communication channels to effectively communicate the key messages.

Public relations communication models set forth by Grunig and Grunig (1992) inform preliminary thoughts about the role of communication in corporate social responsibility; however, communication scholars have advanced these preliminary models into the current dialogic era. Grunig and Grunig's models include a publicity model, a public information model, a two-way asymmetric model, and a two-way symmetrical model. Grunig and Grunig's two-way symmetrical view of communications calls for an act of communication to the receiver and a subsequent return of a message to the sender from the recipient to propel dialogue and change. Scholars have stated that two-way symmetrical communication is the most ethical form of communication (Huang, 2004). Huang (2004) stated that through ethical communication, the company can communicate effectively and achieve desired outcomes that include brand building, reputation enhancement, product trial, and collaboration with communities. The incorporation of symmetrical communication into the discipline of public relations has been guided by ethical dimensions. The public relations industry creates venues for active dialogue and systems adaptation that have the capacity to transform social, economic, and political spheres. Kent and Taylor (1998) indicated that the relationship between two-way symmetrical communication and dialogic communication may be viewed as a difference between process and product.

Scholars have called for the expansion of the ethical, symmetrical communication paradigm across the globe, as the need for transparent communication is required to establish the mutually beneficial relationships across cultures (Kruckeberg, 1996; Newsom, 2001). Kent and Taylor (2002) indicated how to incorporate dialogue into the public relations practice by building interpersonal relationships, building mediated dialogic relationships, and developing procedures for ethical communication. The pair further set forth guidelines of dialogic communication in public relations including dimensions of mutuality, empathy, propinquity, risk, and commitment. Propinquity includes aspects of immediacy of presence and engagement while empathy encompasses the notion of communal orientation (Kent & Taylor, 2002). These aspects remain relevant in studies of CSR communication, particularly within a social media environment, allowing the corporation to depict an "immediacy of presence" and a communal orientation to a specific cause. With the myriad issues regarding social media, relationship marketing, and the fact that individuals now broadcast preferences to consumers via their own technology devices, stakeholder-to-stakeholder communication is captivating researchers as they explore the impact of artificial intelligence and misinformation in various channels. Other scholars agree and are calling for new stream of thought in the stakeholder model. Much of the current thinking in stakeholder theory is still tied to the classic hub-and-spoke model, in which the stakeholders are distinct and mutually exclusive. However, there is a growing consensus that a firm's constituents are actually embedded in interconnected networks of relationships through which the actions of a firm reverberate with both direct and indirect consequences (Bhattacharya & Korschun, 2008). It is in the strength of these consumer-to-consumer relations that power resides. Corporations no longer command complete control over the messages that are disseminated about their company. With the advent of online resources, the Internet and social media sites have made corporations beholden to new delicate communications relationships. The public relations professional now may function to build a community and effectively communicate. The new era of stakeholder-to-stakeholder communication underscores the role of leader, one who can create meaningful dialogue and create a system for communication.

Communicating CSR with an Ethical Posture

Public relations professionals operate in an atmosphere of business and professional ethics. Scholars have called for the incorporation of an expanded ethical model of public relations to incorporate both personal and professional ethics into the CSR realm (Bivins, 1993; Fitzpatrick & Gauthier 2011). Daugherty (2001) also set forth a paradigm for the public relations professional in CSR, citing the communitarian theory and Grunig's two-way symmetrical model. Public relations practitioners have also performed a self-assessment role, finding that their role is sometimes strategic but more often viewed as a tactical communicator (Kim & Reber, 2008). For corporations to yield the maximum benefit from the professional communicator, it is vital for the public relations professional to shed the perception of a singular dimension—that of the publicity agent. Business executives have lagged in understanding this role of the strategic communicators. Yet public relations professionals have a fulsome approach to the marketplace.

CSR activities provide an opportunity for corporate brand building, reputation enhancement, and the solid formation of bonds with key stakeholders. Corporations today often utilize corporate social responsibility initiatives as a component of brand building. Systematic, well-planned, executed, and overtly communicated corporate social responsibility initiatives may contribute to the overall corporate reputation. Scholars urge companies to devise CSR programs that align with the core corporate strategy. Yet businesses navigate troubled waters when they attempt to define programs that resonate with stakeholders and do not create perceptions of "greenwashing" or self-promotion. Contemporary scholarship addresses strategic CSR within the context of marketing, strategic communication, and brand management. The emergence of social media has given rise to a potentially greater role for the consumer in conveying CSR information. The role of the public relations professional must be addressed as the corporate communicator faces the challenge of articulating CSR programs, enfranchising consumer stakeholders, and building a community around corporations. Porter and Kramer (2003) recommend a strategic approach to corporate social responsibility that will enhance the corporation's marketplace position, support the corporate brand, and allow the company to achieve desired business objectives. The pair defined four elements of competitive context that should be incorporated into a corporate social responsibility program: factor conditions such as human resources and infrastructure; context for strategy and rivalry; consideration of related and supporting industries; and demand conditions (Porter & Kramer, 2003). CSR programs with a built-in strategy will promote viability, reinforce facets of the organization, and make future behavior more predictable (Dowling & Moran, 2012). In an analysis of various corporations, Dowling and Moran (2012) differentiate between "bolted-on" versus "built-in" corporate responsibility programs contributing to corporate reputation, indicating that a built-in program is preferable. For communicators, this suggests the need to be present at the decision-making table to create programs. Strategy-based reputation requires leadership and vigilance from all managers responsible for the key business function and must be integrated into corporate operations. Other scholars agree that companies can "do well by doing good" by carefully considering the impact of corporate social responsibility programs on all stakeholders, including shareholders (Falck & Heblich, 2007). Marketing literature has addressed the role of CSR in stakeholder engagement (Bhattacharya & Sen, 2003). Scholars have attempted to categorize different types of corporate social responsibility programs, and Pirsch et al. (2007) delineated between institutionalized programs and promotional programs. Institutionalized programs promoted customer loyalty, enhanced attitude toward the corporation, and decreased skepticism, while promotional ones generated purchase intent (Pirsch et al., 2007). The corporation's point of view regarding corporate social responsibility can lead to negative or positive brand perceptions. Consumers are taking these perceptions to the street by using social media and persuading peers.

THE CORPORATE SOCIAL RESPONSIBILITY/ CORPORATE BRAND REPUTATION NEXUS

Let's examine the corporate social responsibility agenda roster. Corporations taking a thoughtful approach to CSR may want to pursue a program that binds stakeholders to the company, allows the company to sell product, and simultaneously supports the brand. The management team may look across the landscape and find a cause or nonprofit organization that is consistent with their brand, product line, or organization values. To avoid corporate social responsibility missteps, management teams may utilize effective research methods and test potential campaigns with consumers prior to formalizing relationships with nonprofit organizations, investing in cooperative activities or placing the brand in a position that may compromise brand value. In particular, management teams should use this research to avoid the dangerous position of a "pet project" of the chief executive officer or company presidents. In this case, an authority figure inside the organization may make the choice to undertake a corporate social responsibility effort that is not strategically sound. Many times, professional communicators are left wringing their hands wondering why and how they are going to make this fit. By keeping a keen focus on the brand attributes and core values, management teams can avoid costly errors and derive that true, meaningful brand impact they desire through a corporate social responsibility effort.

Academic research indicates a connection between brand building and corporate social responsibility (Bhattacharya et al., 2009). Corporate social responsibility provides a business with aspects of reputation risk management and marketing prowess, if communicated accurately to key stakeholders in a way that resonates with them (Jahdi & Acikdilli, 2009; Vallaster et al., 2012). Werther and Chandler (2005) have called CSR "global brand insurance" to protect against management lapses. Yet to truly invest in the insurance, corporations must develop a program that resonates with stakeholders. Vallaster et al. (2012) state that corporate social responsibility activities must be based on overall brand value and incorporate a theme that resonates with all stakeholder groups. The danger of a forced incongruity of corporate social responsibility activities can result in feelings of mistrust and deception, thus damaging the brand (Vallaster et al., 2012). Corporate leadership must evaluate the nature of the industry, the company's specific product offerings, and the corporate culture and ethos to determine a CSR program that will promote the corporate brand and reputation. Diermeier (2011) has underscored the reputational benefit to companies as corporations undertake ethical and social concerns. Diermeier (2011) points to the fact that using a CSR approach as a reputation strategy assumes that a significant segment of stakeholders respects moral values and is willing and able to support a program. Through this support, the corporation can gain a competitive advantage by satisfying a demand for virtue. Coombs and Holladay (2012) point to CSR as a common point of reference that aligns the corporation's identity, stakeholder identity, and institutional corporate reputation.

When considering the benefits to the corporate brand, a corporate social responsibility campaign may go even further and provide a distinct competitive advantage to the corporation, differentiating its products and services from others in the marketplace. Consider two competing coffee companies—one with a CSR campaign that delivers a competitive advantage, and one that does not. By peeling back to the layers on a strategic corporate social responsibility program, we can see that the program yields exponential benefits. Let's examine a retail coffee company's corporate social responsibility program that offers customers a recycled cup that patrons can carry from the store after the initial purchase and bring back with them each time they purchase a new cup of coffee offered at a reduced price. This program delivers multipronged benefits to the company. First, customers experience a "feel good feeling" that the company is taking action to reduce waste and the carbon footprint. Second, customers appreciate the reduced price and are willing to return to the store, stimulating repeat purchase. Third, the company diminishes the amount of paper cup waste in the store, lowering the workload for retail store employees. Fourth, the company experiences an increase in brand awareness and simultaneously attaches positive brand attributes of being environmentally friendly and customer focused. Overall, this is a win-win situation for the company and the consumer, indicating a strategic corporate social responsibility campaign in action.

The presence of corporate social responsibility programs seems directly linked with corporate reputation. An academic study of 292 large corporations reveals that social responsiveness was one of eight attributes used by consumers to gather information about a company (Fombrun & Shanley, 1990). Findings indicated that publics assign higher reputations to firms that have philanthropic foundations and generously provide to charity (Fombrun & Shanley, 1990). In an analysis of fifty-seven global brands in ten countries, Torres et al. (2012) report CSR is a primary component of brand equity and should be part of the outreach to multiple stakeholder groups. The research divides brand equity into the three parts of customer-based, company-based, and financially-based, and goes on to assert that CSR programs that combine visibility for customers and promote credibility with their community have a stronger effect on marketing metrics like global brand equity (Torres et al., 2012). Corporations operate in a global economy yet require a local market presence for CSR activities that resonates with people on a local level. The brand may also face a risk from irresponsible corporate social behavior. Sweetin et al. (2012) found consumers dealing with socially irresponsible brands are more likely to punish and less likely to reward a corporation than consumers exposed to other types of brands. The study found consumers hold a more positive attitude toward a socially responsible corporate brand and that purchase intention is considerably lower for a socially irresponsible brand (Sweetin et al., 2012). Yet research has also shown that the effective use of CSR communication to inform customers subsequently empowers the corporation and allows the organization to foster public support (Jiang & Park, 2022).

So, when the question to fortify a socially responsible brand emerges, companies are faced with the challenge of analyzing what actions to take that will seem authentic to the brand. If a company develops a program that appears as self-serving or simply "greenwashing," the company can experience a backlash from the marketplace. The motives for a corporate social responsibility campaign emerge from the ethos of the corporation. While stockholders and employees clamor for greater profitability, a CSR campaign may come into question. This obstacle may require management teams to further explore the strategic dimensions of a proposed corporate social responsibility campaign to make sure that it can fulfill the promises of enhancing the brand, promoting customer loyalty, and consequently delivering results for the bottom line. Skepticism about the corporate social responsibility program can harm reputational equity, decrease consumer resistance to negative information, and stimulate unfavorable word-of-mouth actions (Skarmeas & Leonidou, 2013). By testing for four different types of motives, including egoistic-driven, values-driven, strategic-driven, and stakeholder-driven, the researchers found that when consumers attribute the formation of a CSR campaign to egoistic- or stakeholder-driven reasons, skepticism increases. However, if it is viewed as a values-driven motive, the growth of skepticism is inhibited (Skarmeas & Leonidou, 2013). Further, if a company chose a high-fit initiative, one that harmonized with its business and the chosen cause, it was viewed as a positive move, rather than one of excessive profiteering (Ellen et al., 2006).

Chapter 2

Overcoming Skepticism with the Trust Factor

A Corporate Social Responsibility Communication Process Model

Inevitably, companies may experience levels of skepticism when a corporate social responsibility program debuts. If the goal of the program is not immediately recognized, key stakeholders may be left wondering why the company chose to create a particular program. The program may represent the outgrowth or a "pet project" of the company's founder or CEO, without a legitimate and strategic tie to the company. At other times, even a strategically sound program can come under fire. When this occurs, skepticism arrives. With the benefit of a robust strategic communication program companies can take steps to minimize skepticism and pave the way for marketplace adoption of the campaign. While scholarly literature indicates corporate social responsibility programs may convey corporate brand attributes (Bhattacharya & Sen, 2003; Coombs & Holladay, 2012), a multitude of questions arise, particularly regarding the role of social media as a channel for conveying corporate communication messages. The cacophony of news, information, and now disinformation can confuse the marketplace and lead to disenfranchisement.

Skepticism of CSR is an area of concern for brand managers who do not want to be accused of greenwashing or advancing CSR programs for ego or profit-driven motives. The medium a corporation uses to communicate tenets of corporate social responsibility contributes to the success or failure of the campaign in resonating with key stakeholders. For example, a study of online newspapers found that reader comments regarding reaction to corporate social responsibility initiatives can be viewed as cynical, if the campaign occurs immediately after a crisis (Cho & Hong, 2008). Further, there is a connection between CSR image advertising and brand reputation (Pomering & Johnson, 2009). The notion of attribution directly influences the discipline of corporate social responsibility as consumers attempt to discern the reason "why" a corporation has chosen to undertake a specific CSR approach.

In an analysis of the relative impact of brand communications on brand equity through social media, as compared to traditional media, researchers found that while traditional media has a stronger impact on brand awareness, social media communications strongly influence brand image (Bruhn et al., 2012). The study, which tested the differences between user-generated social media content and company-created social media content, found user-generated media communication exerts a major influence on brand image (Bruhn et al., 2012). The link between corporate social responsibility and communication must be addressed to uncover aspects of brand awareness achieved through corporate social responsibility programs with a social media presence. This text encompasses a discussion of the role of the public relations professional, who assumes a leadership role in strengthening the corporate brand and reputation through strategic communication initiatives such as corporate social responsibility programs. Mitigating brand risks may also be managed by the public relations professional, as research has shown media attention can be a catalyst for initiating a corporate social responsibility effort (Zyglidopoulos et al., 2011). In an analysis of the relationship between public relations and its ability to influence perceived corporate reputation, Kiousis et al. (2011) call for public relations professionals to plan strategies to enhance corporate image through social citizenship. With all of these CSR/brand reputation factors, a professional communicator offers tremendous value.

The role of the consumer is also explored in this text because corporations face a new era of brand "co-creation" catalyzed by the prevalence of social media. The door for consumer brand ambassadors is wide open based on the ubiquity of social media. The role of the corporate communicator is evolving too, as corporations come to grips with less managerial control over brand attributes and communication of CSR initiatives. Consequently, marketers can expect that brand communication will cease to be generated solely by the company, but increasingly by the consumers themselves through so-called user-generated social media communication. Therefore, it is crucial to differentiate between firm-created and user-generated social media communication and examine the impact of these two forms of social media communication separately. Scholars point to the use of social media in CSR campaigns, further supporting the approach taken in this text to present content in a social media environment, revealing the CSR/brand connection, as manifested through social media.

The impact of the coronavirus in 2019 brought new challenges to corporations and promoted a sense of urgency for corporations to devise and implement a multitude of corporate social responsibility campaigns. Corporations and consumers found themselves in a global crisis caused by a health pandemic that catalyzed change throughout families and communities. Under this pressure, management teams were dealing with everything from hunger to shelter and significant needs for technology, access to immunizations, and recovery methods. With these aspects in mind, companies were thrust into a broadened leadership position as they faced safety concerns from employee and customers all while coping with the mental well-being of the broader community. Smart companies were able to simultaneously address the short-term needs of the company while contemplating the longer-term impact of the coronavirus and the corresponding impact on the business model and various constituencies.

In the coronavirus era, audiences witnessed collaborations between pharmaceutical companies to bring new vaccinations to market to address the coronavirus pandemic. As the pandemic broadened and spread with new variants, corporations found themselves communicating with government entities and nonprofit organizations to educate community residents about the pandemic, vaccine protocols, employment procedures, and safe work environments. While encountering a global pandemic, some corporations heeded the call to a greater leadership position while others assumed a position of victimhood and did not successfully care for stakeholders with a strategic corporate social responsibility approach. The influence and global penetrating power of the social media industry are virtually unstoppable. The corporate world must accept this power, deploy social media for its communication strategies, and, above all, use it as a CSR branding and firm branding tool and medium. Likewise, CSR is no more than an occasional charity service rendered to local communities, but can be a powerful brand, reaching the millions world over. Consumers are emerging as pivotal authors of brand stories derived as they participate in consumer networks and formulate brands via social media.

A NEW MODEL FOR CORPORATE SOCIAL RESPONSIBILITY COMMUNICATION

The intersection of corporate social responsibility and communication is a topic that has been addressed by scholars who have posed suggestions for corporate communication techniques (Coombs & Holladay, 2012), recommendations for co-creation of content with users (Korschun & Du, 2013), and pleas to incorporate stakeholders into the communication process (Bhattacharya et al., 2011). This book proposes a new five-phase model for CSR communication: Phase 1, strategic CSR investigation and program creation; Phase 2, communications planning (SFS Equation); Phase 3, communication deployment; Phase 4, co-creation with audience; and Phase 5, communication measurement. This model advances a previous CSR process model created by Coombs and Holladay (2012) that called for scanning and monitoring, formative research, creation of CSR initiative, communication of the CSR initiative, evaluation, and feedback. The new model presented in this study considers communication of the CSR program in greater detail and addresses the contemporary social media environment, where dialogic communication and co-creation can occur to influence consumer perceptions of corporate social responsibility. The structure of the new model also advances the management process of public relations set forth by Broom (2009) that calls for four phases: defining public relations problems, planning and programming, taking action and communicating, and evaluating the program. Lastly, the model integrates a communication measurement phase that subscribes to the globally accepted Barcelona Principles, an international guideline for public relations measurement.

THE TRUST FACTOR: CORPORATE SOCIAL RESPONSIBILITY COMMUNICATION PROCESS MODEL

Phase 1: Strategic CSR Investigation and Program Creation

With a seat in the dominant coalition, the public relations professional has a voice in the creation of a corporate social responsibility initiative. Coombs and Holladay (2009) have suggested that the incorporation of the public relations professional at this level is a way to institutionalize the practice into corporate social responsibility. Public relations professionals deliver a keen familiarity of the stakeholder base to the planning process and offer strategic input about the formation and structure of a CSR program. Further, as Bivins (1993) indicates, the public relations professional is in the most favorable position to effect change. As Porter and Kramer (2003) suggested, the formation of a meaningful CSR program must adequately address business results and be founded on a core process of the company. The investigation of the appropriate CSR program requires an analysis of the core business to determine the desired impact on the corporation. For example, a business may be seeking to enhance the corporate reputation, stimulate purchase intention, or achieve another business objective. The program's structure will reflect the business objectives. As Elkington (1997) has stated, corporations today are

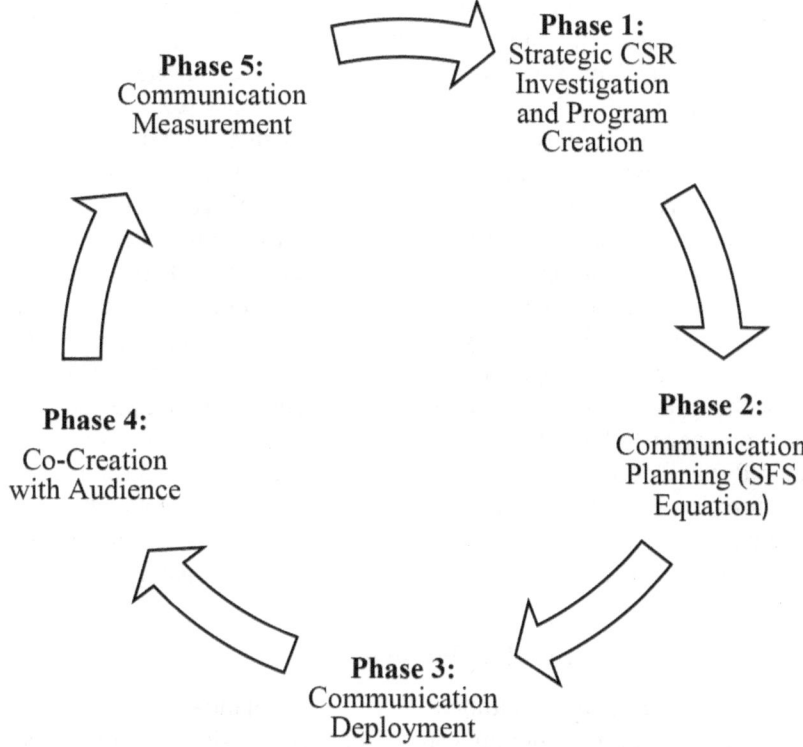

Figure 2.1. The Trust Factor: Corporate Social Responsibility Communication Process Model presents five distinct phases encompassing corporate social responsibility communication program creation, planning, deployment, co-creation with audience, and communication measurement. The communication planning phase includes the SFS Equation, considering the source of the message, the media format used, and the presence of an endorsement sentiment from the source. *Created by the author.*

cognizant of people, planet, and profits, what has come to be known as the "triple bottom line." It has also been suggested that CSR programs can fall along a continuum from institutionalized programs to promotions (Pirsch et al., 2007). Further, when considered as a long-range plan of action, CSR programs offer a way for both companies and society to prosper (Falck & Heblich, 2007). The strategic planning for CSR program planning requires an in-depth analysis of the business objectives and the specific stakeholders that will be reached by the program.

Phase 2: Communication Planning (SFS Equation)

Once a decision has been made about the structure of a corporate social responsibility program, communication planning may commence. This planning must include the evaluation of source, format, and sentiment (SFS) equation. As Basu and Palazzo (2008) have suggested, corporate social responsibility can lend itself to aspects of corporate sensemaking through linguistic dimensions. The selection of the appropriate source, format, and use of sentiment may play a role in the success of the CSR program. The visible source plays a role in influencing the credibility judgment (Dou et al., 2012) and the content class may also serve as a cognitive cue for processing of information (Hallahan, 1999). This model calls for the consideration of these variables and appropriate planning. It has been found corporations that want to enhance the corporate brand reputation, promote purchase, and be viewed as credible source conveying credible information that can be shared via social media should opt for transmitting relevant content. An important role for the SFS Equation is to determine the source, format, and sentiment, but the message must also be developed appropriately so that it resonates with stakeholder audiences. During the planning of the SFS Equation, the public relations executive may work closely with senior management and serve as a liaison with other divisions such as finance and operations to create the structure for the implementation of the corporate social responsibility program.

Phase 3: Communication Deployment

After appropriate source, sentiment, and format planning, a strategic corporate communication program can commence considering the corporate objectives, the key stakeholders, and the recommended tactical approaches. The public relations professional, playing an active role in content creation of news releases, may perform the publicity function for the business, allowing the "story" of the company's corporate social responsibility program to be told in print (newspapers and magazines), broadcast (television and radio), and online media outlets (social media outlets and blogs). Daugherty (2001) has indicated that public relations practitioners must foster mutually beneficial relationships with all stakeholders to achieve harmony. However, a legitimacy gap can occur when a company doesn't meet society's expectations and thus companies function best when they merge their interest with those of stakeholders. But not only must the company merge the interests, but the corporations must also communicate the actions taken to inform and persuade stakeholders. A robust public relations program should be developed and implemented over time. This program may include news media relations, special events, and development of online and social media materials to convey the CSR program and involvement of key stakeholders. Management may not expect instant results in changing perceptions of the corporate brand reputation or purchase intention, but rather may expect a moving of the needle when audiences receive information about the corporate social responsibility program. It has been suggested by Freitag (2005) that the public relations professional specifically target aspects of Carroll's pyramid structure of CSR encompassing legal, economic, ethical, and philanthropic initiatives, by formulating CSR programs and appropriate strategies. Channel planning for a CSR program must fully investigate the media habits of stakeholders. For example, a shareholder investor may receive information in a different content form than an environmental activist consumer. Ongoing monitoring is required to ensure that the communication program is achieving desired objectives. Through careful observation, the corporation can determine if a relationship between the corporation and the consumer is being adequately developed, as this was found advantageous for CSR communications (Hall, 2006). As a primary sculptor of the CSR message, the public relations professional operating in this phase updates senior management and provides recommendations for campaign changes.

Phase 4: Co-Creation with Audience

Once corporate social responsibility information is communicated to the audience, the stage is set for co-creation. Corporations can incentivize consumers to transmit news releases and articles by sending a personal message to them. This activity fuels electronic word of mouth, engages the stakeholder, and strengthens the bond of constituencies involved in the corporate social responsibility program. This dialogic aspect of corporate social responsibility communication has been made possible by the social media channels that proliferate content via engagement activities such as "liking," "sharing," and "posting." Consumers today can take the role of active brand advocates and key influencers persuading others to adopt particular beliefs or reject others. While corporations remain as primary advocates of their own CSR message, the research underscores the stakeholder theory of corporate communication. Without enfranchising stakeholders to engage with the corporation, both as a receiver and relayer of information, the corporation misses an opportunity for dynamic communication. Morsing & Schultz (2006) have indicated that companies benefit most from co-creation of corporate social responsibility, as he advocated a stakeholder involvement strategy that allows for "sensemaking" and "sense giving." Korschun and Du (2013) have provided a framework for CSR dialogue in the social media sphere leading to immediate outcomes of community participation and formation of a CSR expectation that can lead to behavioral outcomes of value for the company. They assert social media fuels co-creation and by uniting social media theory and CSR theory, stakeholder relationships can be improved.

Phase 5: Communication Measurement

Effective measurement of communication outcomes for the corporate social responsibility program is imperative. As Argenti (2006) has stated, corporate communications must measure and quantify business results so that it is not viewed as an amorphous activity. The Barcelona Principles have been routinely updated by the AMEC, the international Association for the Measurement and Evaluation of Communication, providing key benchmarks for monitoring a CSR communication program (AMEC, 2022). The Barcelona Principles assert the following principles: setting goals is an absolute prerequisite to communications planning, measurement, and evaluation; measurement and evaluation should identify outputs, outcomes, and potential impact; outcomes and impact should be identified for stakeholders, society, and the organization; communication measurement and evaluation should include both qualitative and quantitative analysis; advertising value equivalencies are not the value of communication; holistic communication measurement and evaluation includes all relevant online and offline channels; and communication measurement and evaluation are rooted in integrity and transparency to drive learning and insights (AMEC, 2022). A best practice for implementing the Barcelona Principles in a corporate social responsibility program allows for corporate goal setting that unites the business objective with stakeholder communication. Media measurement may be conducted that involves quality and quantity by employing both internal and external measurement techniques. For example, a business may form a relationship with an external monitoring company to determine levels of coverage, conduct focus group research with key stakeholders, and establish an internal operating framework that includes active review of materials for effectiveness. According to the Barcelona Principles, advertising value equivalencies are not a sound method for monitoring public relations effectiveness. This study has further shown that that advertising is not a preferable media format for conveying CSR information in the social media environment. For measurement of social media, a company may undertake an active listening approach and employ a third-party vendor for scanning of public conversations about the corporation or can purchase software that would allow the monitoring to occur in real time. The public relations industry has endured criticism for measuring outputs often in the form of a news release, media interview, special event, or other activity. While monitoring of this type is important for management, the measurement of outcomes is more important as it ties back to corporate goals. A business can measure the products sold as a result of a CSR campaign or measure the change in corporate brand reputation that occurs during and after the implementation of a CSR program. The imperative remains for corporate communicators to directly document the impact of communication on business results. The precise nature of online communication allows this type of business impact substantiation to be more readily available to executives making decisions about CSR programs. Lastly, measurement must be transparent and replicable, corporations conducting CSR programs can develop internal best practices for measurement and adopt a culture of replication that allows for sustaining corporate social responsibility programs though years. By measuring corporate social responsibility communication with these robust standards, companies can identify gaps and retool programs to effectively resonate with stakeholders.

Businesses undertaking corporate social responsibility do so for a variety of business reasons. As scholars have found and practitioners have implemented, the development of a corporate social responsibility program must be a strategic undertaking that incorporates core business dimensions. Pirsch et al. (2007) have indicated that institutionalized CSR programs can influence purchase intentions. In a similar vein, Vallaster et al. (2012) have indicated that a corporate brand is best served by having an engrained attitude to corporate social responsibility rather than a "bolted-on" approach. While we examine the connection between a corporate reputation and a corporate social responsibility program, we find a solid opportunity for strategic communication. With the inclusion of the public relations professional from the outset of the planning process, the company invests in future stakeholder trust by making sure that communication will accurately and authentically present the brand to the marketplace. Through communication, the team may exercise dialogic communication with key stakeholders, further solidifying the company/stakeholder bond. We accurately observe the move from sender-receiver models to more dialogic ones, as social media fuels interactive conversations about CSR programs. We recognize that at times, skepticism can occur, but the implementation of a holistic communication model to advance the process will help to reduce potential negative feedback. The five-phase communication model contained in this chapter addresses aspects of CSR program creation, program planning, communication deployment, co-creation with the audience, and communication measurement.

Chapter 3

A Credible Source to Carry the Corporate Social Responsibility Message

The presence of a global pandemic immediately brought companies to a new era of communication. Businesses were forced to communicate across the miles and face new challenges with the use of technology and mediated communications. Corporations and professional communicators engaged in corporate social responsibility face the daunting challenge to find the right communicator to effectively carry the message to multiple audiences. They grapple with the issue, who should carry the message, a CEO, a communications professional, a celebrity spokesperson, or someone else? This chapter explores the conundrum that professional communicators face when charged with communicating a corporate social responsibility program and provides insight on how to appropriately carry the message.

THE ROLE OF THE CORPORATE COMMUNICATOR

Professional communicators charged with CSR must assess the availability of communication channels and explore the effectiveness of potential carriers of the message. Traditional marketing channels and social networking represent topline approaches to CSR communication, but a thoughtful communicator will go even deeper to contemplate how the message receiver will attribute the information and act on the data. We can observe a link between the message carrier and the medium chosen. Marketing communication tools often play a major role in conveying a company's CSR message, and corporations must choose the appropriate media format for the target audience (Jahdi & Acikdilli, 2009). Corporations striving for strategic communication must address the appropriate methods for boosting audience receptiveness and then communicate with them in the most advantageous way. Companies seek to engage stakeholders and prompt them to take action. Researchers have found that content class influences consumers and the amount of effort they are willing to exert to process information, thus having an impact on the level of persuasion that can be achieved (Hallahan, 1999). A study examining the influences of public relations efforts, media coverage, public opinion, and financial performance discovered a positive relationship between corporate media relations messages and corporate social responsibility, indicating that communication via public relations activities may be a preferred solution for corporations (Kiousis et al., 2011). Yet who is carrying the message, a professional communicator or the chief executive officer? When a corporation seeks to inform the desired audience about a corporate social responsibility program, researchers have found that priming and framing activities may promote persuasive effects. Further, the preconceived notions and positions an individual holds toward the company influences the persuasive effect in each case (Wang, 2011). This phenomenon leads researchers to conclude that public relations practitioners should make strategic decisions about priming and framing, and course-correct, as appropriate (Wang, 2011).

The ubiquity of social networking sites presents a new landscape for corporate social responsibility communicators, and companies must strive for highly credible communication to offset stakeholder criticism of CSR programs (Bhattacharya et al., 2011). When choosing a channel to communicate, companies must be aware of the trade-offs of complete control exercised by using their own channels and the sacrificed control that occurs by allowing external sources to convey messages. There is likely to be a trade-off between the controllability and credibility of CSR communication; the less controllable the communicator is, the more credible it is and vice versa. Stakeholders will likely perceive the company focused more on self-interest when they learn about its CSR primarily through company sources compared to noncorporate sources (Bhattacharya et al., 2011, p. 203). Yet, despite these risks, Bhattacharya et al. (2011) advocate the use of word-of-mouth communication about CSR because stakeholders are more likely to trust these messages than those sent directly from the company. Coombs and Holladay (2012) advance this argument by stating that by enfranchising all stakeholders in a CSR communication to function as message carriers in social media and word-of-mouth realms, an "echo" will be created that allows stakeholders to do the communicating for the corporation. This concept is based on early mass communication research by Katz and Lazarsfield (1955). They coined the two-step flow of communication that indicates mass media's effect on people occurred through opinion leaders. We now actively observe the two-step flow of communication from the corporation to the consumer, who may ultimately decide to convey corporate information to a third party. Attribution theory also plays a role as consumers apply meaning to the information based on the media format and source.

Literature regarding corporate social responsibility has indicated that stakeholders' response may respond to CSR initiatives based on their own anticipated rewards or benefits (Bhattacharya et al., 2011), and that consumers attempt to attribute reasons why the corporation undertakes a corporate social responsibility campaign (Vlachos et al., 2009). With this information in mind, it is important to note that the source will play a vital role in the credibility of information transmitted about a corporate social responsibility campaign.

Research suggests that consumers attempt to attribute the reason why a corporation has undertaken a corporate social responsibility campaign (Pomering & Johnson, 2009). The consumer's evaluation of the company's reputation and brand can vary as it assesses firm-generated content and user-generated content, suggesting a multitude of outcomes for brand perception (Bruhn et al., 2012). For example, an individual may trust the information coming from a friend, but question the marketing campaign from the company to support a CSR program. To probe further, the perceptions of advertising messages conveyed from a consumer or from the corporation may influence brand attitude in different manners. The source, format, and sentiment attached to a corporate social responsibility campaign represent a confluence of factors that can influence the way a consumer interprets the corporate brand. Research suggests that programs that harmonize with the core values of the consumer will resonate well with them and deliver positive business results (Ellen et al., 2006). Further, it has been asserted that global brand equity may be influenced by corporate social responsibility activities (Torres et al., 2012). Therefore, it should be noted that the source of the communication plays a vital role, as does the perception gleaned by the consumer. For public relations professionals, it is important to consider where the message comes from and what is stated (in both verbal and written forms) to reach key stakeholders.

The origin of communication presents a primary concern for corporate and individual communicators. The credibility of the source can lead to support for specific arguments or contribute to rejection of the message by the recipient. From the perspective of ancient orators, Aristotle set forth the communication triangle encompassing the pathos, logos, and ethos aspects of persuasion to explain source dynamics (Kennedy, 2007). These tenets continue to enlighten common communication challenges such as the one presented in this study. While Hovland and Weiss (1951) addressed source effectiveness and found that individuals may discount messages from untrustworthy sources, multiple perspectives of the corporate source (Argenti, 2009) and the consumer source (Kim, 2011) have emerged in the area of corporate social responsibility communication. During Covid-19, right-wing activists called the credibility of scientists into question as they questioned the pandemic's severity. Many corporations assumed a leadership role by demanding that employees get tested for Covid-19 and undergo immunizations. The viral spread of information influenced the interpretation of the pandemic and allowed businesses to use a multitude of social media channels to communicate about corporate social responsibility and stimulate engagement with the company. Research in this area has suggested that various source/media format combinations can directly contribute to purchasing decisions (Byrum, 2017).

IMPACT ON THE ROLE OF THE PUBLIC RELATIONS PROFESSIONAL

Contemporary public relations professionals remain concerned about communicating with key publics in the most effective way. Effective communication influences the success or failure of a CSR program. The public relations profession has continued to underscore the compelling need for dialogic communication with key stakeholders. When the dialogue occurs, aspects of the campaign can be revealed and skepticism quelled. These implications pave the way for a deeper understanding of the role of the public relations professional in formulating and executing a strategic communication program for corporate social responsibility initiatives. As the public relations industry moves beyond traditional sender and receiver models to a new era of dialogic communication, the consumer plays a more active role. Worley (2007) has suggested that the Internet has become a great "equalizer" for person-to-person communication. To effectively communicate with consumers and incentivize them to engage in the corporate social responsibility program, public relations professionals can subscribe to the tenets of communitarian theory set forth by Starck and Kruckeberg (2001). In the case of Covid-19 communications, public relations professionals utilized their own social media channels to share thoughts on the pandemic and information about resources and spread corporate social responsibility campaigns. Consistent with the communitarian theory, corporations can be both moral and profitable at the same time, and communication plays a significant role in building stakeholder relationships. In addition, by incorporating dialogic principles advocated by Kent and Taylor (1998), the public relations professional can conduct a strategic communications process that allows organizations to form mutually beneficial relationships with key publics, as stated in the definition of public relations (PRSA, 2022). Corporate social responsibility programs are unable to have any real lifespan without the work of professional communicators. The best public relations pros breathe life into CSR programs by creating dialogues between a program's creators and a company's employees and C-suite, journalists, the public at large on digital channels, and communities that stand to benefit from the program. A CSR campaign cannot be sustained without such dialogues.

An Evolved Role for the Public Relations Officer

While at times companies choose to isolate CSR communication to a separate department, the public relations professional offers unique and meaningful insights, as many professionals understand the demographics and motivational drivers of the key stakeholders in the corporate social responsibility communication process. To solidify the argument that the public relations professional is in a prime position to communicate CSR, consider several noteworthy aspects of the profession. First, public relations meets the standards of a profession including (1) a specialized education system, (2) a unique body of knowledge ground in theoretical research, (3) independence, (4) recognition by a community, and (5) governance by a code of ethics (Broom, 2009). These aspects of professionalism bolster the argument for the role of the public relations professionals as leaders and communicators of CSR. The public relations professional is an ethical communicator, suited for the role in corporate social responsibility. The Public Relations Society of America (PRSA), the largest global professional organization of public relations practitioners, provides an ethics code that encompasses ethical values and provides conduct recommendations. The code's values include advocacy, honesty, independence, loyalty, and fairness in the communication of messages. The conduct recommendations include protecting the free flow of information and promoting transparency. These ethical considerations guide public relations practitioners today as they undergo accreditation and practice strategic communication for organizations each day. The maturation of the discipline as a profession, the existence of the ethical code, and the incorporation of contemporary ethical theories to the profession provide a foundation for the involvement of the strategic communicator in CSR. In a call for incorporation of the public relations professional into the CSR process, Clark cites the unique capacity of public relations professionals, stating that they have a keen ability to scan the political, social, and historic environments, delivering solid perspectives to corporate social responsibility programs (Clark, 2000).

With a focus on ethical communication delivered in a way that resonates with the contemporary media consumer, the communication process emerges as a tool for community building. Dialogues occur everywhere, both in the online world and offline, allowing public relations professionals to thrive as they determine the right messages and the media channels. Public relations professionals are stepping into a new role as facilitators of electronic word of mouth, serving not only as creators and disseminators of the message, but also as conduits for community building. To better understand the strategic dimension of communication, Argenti (2005) states that a management imperative exists to incorporate communication professionals into the top levels of decision-making. Argenti interviewed CEOs of top US companies and concluded that strategic communication was a missing link, because professional communicators lacked the measurement of business outcomes. Strategic communicators must provide appropriate measurement that contributes to the business decision-making of the organization. In fact, Argenti (2006) argues that when senior managers recognize communications, they connect with corporate strategy and can assist with executing on the business model. For professional communicators to truly deliver the value of communication they must have access to the decision-making table.

Unfortunately, many business leaders still subscribe to an outdated view of the public relations professional in one narrow role as a "publicity agent." In a study of 173 public relations professionals, they were asked to characterize their role in CSR in one of the following categories: significant management, philanthropic, value-driven communication, and none. Coombs and Holladay (2009) argue that CSR is a door to the dominant coalition of executive management and advocate that two-way communications is the best way to understand and adapt to stakeholder concerns. Instead of considering communication as an "afterthought," public relations professional methodically planning a corporate social responsibility communication initiative are uniquely suited to lead corporate social responsibility efforts. While communication is important, it seems that decisions about the role of communication are made by top leaders and can mean the difference between inclusion or exclusion. Kim and Reber (2008) found that the contributions of public relations professionals were limited by the acceptance of top managers to CSR. While managers may view a CSR program as significant and managerial, practitioners often lacked influence and final authority and were relegated to a publicity-based communication role. This misperception stems from the publicity heritage of the profession. Benn et al. (2010) have documented this phenomenon and have called for model of distributive leadership that allows cultures to change with the support of top management. Since the public relations industry has evolved from traditional press agentry roots, contemporary public relations professionals now have the ability to strategically communicate with multiple stakeholders. Public relations professionals choose messages, devise communication techniques, and select venues to carry corporate messages inside the organization and beyond the walls to investors, customers, society, the supply chain, government regulators, and others. It can be asserted that the strategic public relations professional deftly discerns the multifaceted aspects of the stakeholders, clearly conveys messages to these diverse stakeholders, establishes two-way communication, and refines message approaches accordingly, allowing adaptation to occur.

AN EVOLVING DISCIPLINE

As corporate social responsibility continues to evolve as a discipline, facing challenges that include the absence of a clear, mutually agreed-upon definition, the role of communication has also encountered murky interpretations about the source and media formats in a corporate social responsibility campaign. The advent of new communication technologies and the transformation of consumer-to-consumer communication in the atmosphere of pervasive social media creates an atmosphere of content co-creation. The role of the public relations professional remains under scrutiny by academic and corporate spheres. In a move from a master technician who disseminates content, the strategic communicator is one who carries messages to multiple stakeholders and fosters the development of two-way communication loops. The public relations professional thus becomes a "community maker," who systematically empowers the community members to articulate corporate messages. By fueling this empowerment and subsequent communication, the corporation thus reaps the benefits of enhanced communication in the consumer-to-consumer loop. Scholarly literature is denoting a shift of the public relations professional beyond the press agentry heritage to a position of the expert prescriber who builds and sustains communities around corporations by leveraging dialogic principles in the social media age.

The communitarian theory of public relations continues to evolve with the advent of new "virtual communities." The theoretical grounding for the argument of increased public relations professional involvement is based in the communitarian theory of public relations as set forth by Starck and Kruckeberg (2001). The researchers evaluated multiple aspects of community and found that public relations practitioners (not tacticians) could serve as creators of community by helping corporations and their communities become conscious of common interests, overcome alienation, and create a sense of community (Kruckeberg et al., 2006). Scholars have also called for embracing communitarian theory as a "metatheory" of public relations (Leeper, 2001). Communitarian theory resonates in the pandemic era because it addresses relationship building as a potential point of union between public relations and corporate social responsibility. Communication operates at the center of pandemic dialogues. This aspect of relationship building is a vital role of the strategic communication professional and also requires greater involvement of the public relations professional in corporate social responsibility. Further, the advent of social media has redefined virtual communities and the word-of-mouth function, formulating the question about the role of the public relations professional in conveying corporate information. This chapter asserts that the public relations professional may engage in a newly evolved role as a community builder through strategic dialogic communication.

The intersection of corporate social responsibility and communication demonstrates a new intersection that leads to trust. While scholars of CSR indicate that linguistic dimensions of CSR may carry dimensions of transparency and justification (Basu & Palazzo, 2008), the receiver plays a dynamic role in "attributing" the rationale for the CSR campaign. The receiver's perception of the source credibility influences these decisions, as the receiver makes ad hoc judgments about the source credibility of the corporate social responsibility information.

Corporations that choose to undertake a CSR program consider the source, the media format, and the message (Coombs & Holladay, 2012). For example, both a corporation and an individual may transmit CSR information in the form of a news release, article, or advertisement via social media. With Covid-19-related communication, we observed friends and thought leaders taking a larger role in sharing information about masks, immunizations, quarantine policies, school policy, government actions, and corporate policies. Dou et al. (2012) have indicated that the visible source plays a role in influencing the credibility judgment. The content class may also serve as a cue for cognitive processing of information (Hallahan, 1999). A message that originates from a corporation versus one that originates with a consumer may have differences in stimulating source credibility. This is particularly interesting as the sender chooses to transmit various media formats including a news release, article, or advertisement, common tools of contemporary corporate social responsibility programs. The content class and the sender influence the ability of the company to gain trust with the end user (Byrum, 2017).

THE ROLE OF ATTRIBUTION BY THE RECEIVER IN CORPORATE SOCIAL RESPONSIBILITY

After conducting the strategic planning and investing resources into the creation of a corporate social responsibility program, a company wants the program to succeed, suggesting that audiences attribute positive aspects to the program and get involved. Corporate social responsibility introduces a new dynamic beyond the simple assessment of trustworthiness of the source and the format, as the audience now attempts to discern or "attribute" the reason why the corporation has undertaken the campaign. Is this campaign profit driven? What is the corporate motivation? Why is the company doing this now? These represent common questions asked by the consumer encountering information about a corporate social responsibility program. Once a message about corporate social responsibility is communicated, information flows into the marketplace of ideas and may be interpreted by the receiver in a positive way or a negative way, or not perceived at all. Research has found that a consumer may investigate the motives of the corporation in developing a corporate social responsibility program, and this discernment can promote a positive or negative perception. Bhattacharya et al. (2011) assert stakeholders respond to CSR initiatives based on their own anticipated rewards or personal benefits. The measurable benefits that can be gained indicate the nature of the stakeholder-company relationship. A stakeholder-centric model has been proposed that indicates stakeholder perceptions of CSR initiatives are based on values, psychosocial benefits, and functional benefits, leading to the formation of a stakeholder-company relationship. This relationship in turn leads to behavioral outcomes such as company-directed behaviors, cause-directed behaviors, and other-stakeholder-directed behaviors (Bhattacharya et al., 2009).

As we consider corporate social responsibility communication, it is relevant to note that some segments of the public are more susceptible to corporate social responsibility messages than others. The character of the individual receiving the information also plays a role in the interpretation. Giacalone et al. (2005) found hopeful people embrace corporate social performance. This is revealed by a relationship between positive psychological dispositions and consumer sensitivity to corporate social performance. It has been found that increased levels of gratitude interact with levels of hope in pro-social behavior to yield increased sensitivity to corporate social performance (Giacalone et al., 2005). In the pandemic world, this can lead to more proactive approaches to citizenship and a belief in the collective society addressing a global health emergency. To further explore whether consumers' perceptions of corporate motives influence their evaluation of corporate social responsibility efforts, Vlachos et al. (2009) tested four types of motives, including ego driven, stakeholder driven, strategic driven, and values driven, to discern the levels of consumer suspiciousness about corporate social responsibility and the corresponding impact on consumer trust. The study found that values-driven attributions yield a positive influence on consumer trust, while ego-driven attributions diminish trust and patronage intentions (Vlachos et al., 2009). When consumers perceive their lifestyle congruent with corporate CSR activities, they consider CSR genuine and favorable, leading to increased customer loyalty (Lee et al., 2012).

So, as we consider the scholarly literature, the theme of attribution arises. Attribution of CSR motives is a common theme found in CSR literature. Dean (2002) found that in a test of attribution theory on a corporate sponsorship program that perceptions are largely mediated through attributional constructs and that corporations are best served by creating a "perceptual fit" between the corporation and sponsor. Researchers have examined the influence of "product fit" in corporate social responsibility, and found that the degree of "fit" between products has a significant effect on consumers' evaluations of products that carry a cause of "brand identity" as part of a customer relationship management (CRM) campaign (Hamlin & Wilson, 2004). For corporate social responsibility then, companies must choose products and programs that harmonize with the belief systems of consumers. Yet this is a complicated problem, particularly as consumers gain information from many sources. To better understand how consumers perform credibility assessments of online information, Metzger (2007) proposes a dual process model that encompasses three phases for exposure, evaluation, and judgment. The exposure phase includes motivation to evaluate and ability to evaluate (Metzger, 2007). Research further suggests trust is a factor in ecommerce and that lack of trust can be a barrier for commercial transactions. Trust may be enhanced by graphic design, structure design, content design, and social cue design (Metzger, 2007). Website design can also compensate for low sponsor credibility (Westerwick, 2013). Corporate social responsibility communicators using online transactional models effectively utilize all aspects of graphic design and messaging to overcome these barriers. The contemporary business atmosphere dictates that corporations devise and implement communication strategies that resonate with key stakeholders, establishing a platform for further study regarding the role of the corporate communicator and the tools selected to communicate corporate social responsibility messages.

TIPS FOR CREATING DIALOGUES IN CORPORATE SOCIAL RESPONSIBILITY CAMPAIGNS

1. Conduct research regarding the social media habits of stakeholders involved with your CSR program: By understanding the media consumption habits of all stakeholder groups, you may successfully incorporate strategies of dialogue. Conduct a social media communications audit that defines each stakeholder group and its typical social media habits.
2. Create an inventory of CSR communications materials based on your message strategy: This is a back-to-basics move that allows you to articulate your key messages for each audience. Typical communications vehicles may include news releases, fact sheets, biographies, statistics, and articles.

3. Plan ahead by creating a calendar of sequential CSR correspondence: As you examine the CSR program rollout, consider the timing of communications to each stakeholder group. Through coordinated timing, you can create a synergistic effect of awareness and engagement. Establish a timeline for communication that may include daily, weekly, and monthly activities to bolster conversation.
4. Use your personal voice and the corporate voice to convey CSR: As a public relations professional, you become a facilitator of dialogue. As a thought leader, you may convey sentiments for meaningful results. By extending beyond the corporate voice, the CSR program gains personality and may promote engagement.
5. Monitor the contemporary environment and seize opportunities: A CSR campaign occurs in a dynamic landscape. Find opportunities to connect with news, trends, and strategic aspects of the company's business to foster dialogue with all stakeholder groups.
6. Leverage technology tools: Based on your social media audit conducted at the beginning of the program, you have gained insight about technology use for your stakeholders. While preferred social media channels may remain at the foundation of your communications program, purposefully integrate emerging technologies to advance dialogues.
7. Reward your CSR community: As the CSR program matures, your community will emerge as a robust source of information and dialogue. You may reward your community by giving it relevant news it can use such as articles, additional facts, CSR program updates, and other content. By encouraging it to share this information in the social media environment, you will further propel engagement with your CSR program.
8. Listen to your CSR stakeholders and measure communications: Before you speak, write, or engage with your community, listen and observe trends. You may utilize social media monitoring tools that will allow you to monitor sentiments regarding specific topics. The dialogue that you create will become a valuable information resource, as you will learn myths and misperceptions that exist about the CSR program, and you will discern the specific key messages resonating with stakeholders. Utilize the Barcelona Principles of PR measurement and routinely evaluate social media monitoring technologies.
9. Adapt your CSR program if dialogic efforts fail: As you endeavor to create a CSR community, the precise timing of messages, use of communications channels, and engagement with stakeholders may stall or fail. If measurement reveals sparse dialogue and the absence of community formation, it's time to devise new message approaches, identify different channels of communication, and explore alternative media outlets.

10. Maintain your own CSR best practices and repeat success: During the campaign, conduct self-assessment, based on your social media monitoring. Evaluate honestly the success of your community-building effort and itemize the sequential steps taken to create your CSR communication best practices.

Chapter 4

Creating and Sharing Credible CSR Information

The imperative to accurately and effectively communicate is born the moment the corporate social responsibility program is established. Communicating the effort, both internally among key stakeholders and externally outside the walls of the corporation to the myriad external audiences that can make the program a success or failure, deserves both attention to detail and an allocation of financial resources in the CSR program budget. Through effective communication, the corporate communicator can develop meaningful relationships with stakeholders. However, the pitfalls of claims of "self-promotion," "untimely messages," or "off-target" communications indicate ongoing threats in the formulation of a CSR stakeholder ecosystem.

Corporate communications officers continuously examine the broad array of media formats to determine the best approach for the initiative, assessing paid media, earned media (as evidenced through news media exposure for the company), shared media (such as the co-creation of user-generated content on social media), and the wealth of owned media channels such as corporate websites, direct marketing programs, social media channels, and other corporate-owned vehicles. As the world tackled the Covid-19 pandemic, we can observe how corporations used these various information channels to communicate with key stakeholders. For example, Dove initiated the Dove Health Hero campaign, recognizing healthcare workers who suffered from skin conditions as the result of wearing protective face masks (Dove, 2022). The evocative campaign generated empathy for the workers yet remained as a solid strategic campaign that was consistent with Dove's effort to promote natural beauty. The campaign utilized all facets of paid, earned, shared, and owned media. The "Courage Is Beautiful" campaign underscored the sacrifices and hard work of actual medical professionals and first responders, highlighting their hard work in the face of adversity. Dove, and the parent company, Unilever, donated millions of dollars of in-kind donations of products such as soap, personal hygiene products, and cleaning products to help with the global fight against the coronavirus pandemic, further demonstrating corporate social responsibility activity.

Health products company Tylenol answered the call to engage with key stakeholders during pandemic. During the early 2020 period that encouraged home quarantine to avoid transmission and exposure to Covid-19, Tylenol produced a series of paid advertisements that encouraged citizens to simply stay home. The campaign, "Stay Home for Health Professionals," revealed vignettes of families at home and healthcare workers on the job. In one segment, healthcare workers, outfitted in personal protective equipment, held up placards that stated, "I stay at work for you, you stay at home for us." The campaign urged viewers to stay healthy, smart, connected, together, and safe. The company utilized multiple communication channels, as the campaign appeared on Instagram, Facebook, and other social media channels. In addition to raising public awareness, Tylenol donated to the American Nurses Foundation coronavirus response fund (Tylenol, 2022)

The Dove and Tylenol campaigns illustrate how corporations successfully analyzed the Covid-19 situation and determined a corporate social responsibility program that was relevant to their business, and could offer a benefit to various stakeholders. The company chose the appropriate media to communicate and utilized trusted sources to carry the message. A multitude of companies have chosen various corporate social responsibility programs to communicate with employees, customers, and their broader communities. In addition to programmatic efforts, companies have also provided in-cash donations during the Covid period, including the $225 million donated by Cisco Systems, $65 million by Citigroup, and $50 million by Johnson and Johnson (Mahmud et al., 2021). The CSR communication landscape remains ever changing, requiring professional communicators to evolve with the changing circumstances. Let's look at the heritage of academic research.

Academic research has shown that varying sources and media channels can have a significant impact on the consumer's perception of the campaign. Media credibility research typically focuses on two main dimensions: source credibility and medium credibility (Golan, 2010). Research regarding source credibility has been accomplished by Hovland and Weiss (1951) and advanced by contemporary researchers who have evaluated online news information (Sundar, 1998), and online advertising information (Greer, 2003). Scholarly literature documents changes in the corporate sphere as enterprises undertake CSR programs. Today, the Covid-19 global pandemic presents new challenges for corporations undertaking corporate social responsibility programs yet the need for communication endures. Many corporations are rethinking corporate social responsibility programs to adapt to the new environment (Carroll, 2021). The pandemic exerts tremendous impact on employees, consumers, and existing charitable organizations, requiring creativity and innovation in CSR. These efforts intersect with research on source and media credibility.

With the fluidity of the pandemic, the public relations professional's role emerges into clear focus. Professional communicators perform a vital role communicating with others, most notably the consumers who are engaged with the brand. Together, they create new programs and give the CSR new life. When corporations undertake a corporate social responsibility initiative, they may do so for a multitude of reasons, including enfranchising stakeholders, promoting the corporate brand, and stimulating purchase of goods and services. The global pandemic places a new veil over all of these activities—calling into question how companies survive, thrive, and meet the needs of a marketplace that is politically polarized, confused, and in need of accurate information. Corporate social responsibility programs provide a way for consumers to engage with a corporation that allows them to elaborate on corporate messages, thus creating a positive or negative perception. During the global pandemic, consumers struggle to understand their immediate world and interpret information through a lens that may be distorted by misinformation and disinformation. Some scholars have asserted that CSR can perform the function of sensemaking and have provided frames for corporate best practices of CSR, explaining how we think about, verbalize, and behave. Basu and Palazzo (2008) have set forth a tripartite model of corporate sensemaking that includes cognitive, linguistic, and conative (behavioral) dimensions, as depicted as what companies think, what firms say, and how firms tend to behave. This has been further broken down into cognitive dimensions of identity orientation and legitimacy, linguistic dimensions of justification and transparency, and conative (behavioral) dimensions of posture, consistency, and commitment (Basu & Palazzo, 2008). These scholars assert that by understanding the internal processes of sensemaking, knowledge can be gained regarding the language used by a corporation to discuss corporate social responsibility and convey such information to the marketplace. For example, when corporations discuss CSR internally, the talks may go to legal, scientific, economic, and ethical arguments. In the midst of the global pandemic, all of these factors converged and corporate decisions were made to preserve and protect the corporation, its employees, and profits so in fact the company can continue operations.

While executives and public relations professionals struggle to implement CSR dimensions, scholars probe new theoretical foundations. For example, four key propositions for CSR theory development have been developed: living corporate social responsibility from the inside out, earning trust of the public and the media, giving back as a community citizen, and accepting that we are all in this together (Spangler & Pompper, 2011). Each of these approaches and theoretical frameworks assume dimensions of communications. In the pandemic, corporations consider how audiences attribute the information to the source and how they perceived the data coming at them. With the global pandemic, Carroll (2021) notes how businesses are making the shift to more strategic CSR, because the impact on the key stakeholders is undeniable.

AUDIENCE ENGAGEMENT

With the world focused on the shared objective of managing the Covid-19 pandemic, the audience assumes a greater role. Consumers stand up and attempt to discern the practicality and usefulness of the corporate social responsibility program. As corporations communicate the corporate social responsibility campaign to key stakeholders, the audience enters a phase of engagement that scholars call attribution. Ellen et al. (2006) characterize the engagement by the consumer as placing the CSR initiative on a "self" and "other" continuum. Specifically, consumers may respond positively to CSR efforts judged as values driven and strategic, while they may respond negatively to ones perceived as stakeholder driven or egoistic by the corporation (Ellen et al., 2006). This approach considers attribution theory and underscores the fact that consumer's attribution of the CSR "reason" plays a role in the response to corporate social responsibility efforts. Scholars of attribution theory view people as "naïve scientists" attempting to gain information to make a causal inference (Folkes, 1988). But if consumers view the CSR program as self-serving and impractical, the audience becomes turned off. A "discounting principle" may emerge if an alternative attribution could account for the behavior and the communicator's credibility may play a role in the discounting principle (Folkes, 1988). Research suggests the attribution of the "reason" why a corporation undertakes a CSR initiative, the media format used to articulate the information, and the source chosen to transmit information may all play a role in the effectiveness of the campaign and the acceptance by the marketplace. Dou et al. (2012) utilized attribution theory as a premise to investigate the role that sources play in influencing an individual's evaluation of online information and concluded that the message presenter, the visible source, influences the credibility judgment of the message originator (Dou et al., 2012). With this in mind, corporations that engage in the Covid-19 dialogue must consider the source and the message to confirm that the CSR campaign does not alienate key publics. Instead, companies want to engender feelings of trust. How receivers attribute the information can mean the success or failure of the campaign. When considering the flow of information about a CSR campaign, it is also important to consider *how* receivers gain the information. To better understand these variables in the global pandemic, let's explore attribution and persuasion in greater detail. Scholars point to an attribution theory phenomenon which has become known as a "sleeper effect." The elaboration likelihood model sets forth the notion that there are two distinct routes for information persuasion, a central route and a peripheral route (Petty & Cacioppo, 1986). The amount of "elaboration," or thinking, put forth by an audience can be placed on a continuum, and consumer motivations can be influenced by multiple variables including perceived personal relevance to an issue (Rucker & Petty, 2006). In other words, if a consumer believes in a particular cause, their elaboration will be higher as they receive communication messages. The concept of elaboration is relevant to studies of corporate social responsibility communication, because the audience may exert personal beliefs and elaboration based on the campaign issue. For example, a consumer may be more in tune with an environmental or health issue, thus easing the routes of persuasion. Rucker and Petty (2006) set forth a plan to evaluate risk communications by specifying a multistep approach that calls for considering the audience elaboration level, designing and evaluating message characteristics, discerning if the message objective is designed to stimulate immediate or enduring attitude change, determining if there is a fit of audience elaboration level, message information, and desired attitude change, testing the message effectiveness, and evaluating the message effectiveness (Rucker & Petty, 2006). Thus, through these examples it is observed that the audience's involvement plays a role in determining the perceived credibility of the source in a corporate social responsibility initiative. Content class has also been studied in relation to the elaboration likelihood model, including a study of the difference between news and advertising characterized as a cue for cognitive processing of a message (Hallahan, 1999). Researchers found people with both high and low involvement were influenced by the content class (Hallahan, 1999). For contemporary practitioners, this means that whether a media relations campaign or a paid advertising program is deployed, the use of the particular channel for communication can directly influence the program's success or failure. Further, source credibility of persuasive messages has an impact both on affective and cognitive responses of message receivers (Li, 2013).

As corporations consider strategic approaches to CSR communication, it is important to recognize the role of the source who functions as the message sender. For the practicing public relations professional, decisions about who carries the message, what they say, and in what channel, become important to determining if the program will yield desired results. In fact, scholars suggest that when conducting empirical research, corporate social responsibility communicators must examine multiple factors simultaneously. For example, Prez et al. (2019) found that consumer responses to CSR communication are influenced by multiple variables, making the communication challenge complex. In the Covid-19 environment, issues related to gender disparity, mental health, and socio-economic difference have come to the fore as businesses communicate with employee stakeholders. So what can an organization do to make that communication better, even it is mediated by the computer and technology-enabled audio and video? The need for branding and corporate ownership over the messages become even more important. It has been found source cues must be presented first to leverage credibility benefits (Sternthal et al., 1978). Moderately credible sources can be more persuasive than highly credible ones when the source credibility cues precede the message. Research has also found that electronic word of mouth relies on source expertise as a factor in determining the effectiveness of persuasive communication (Coulter & Roggeveen, 2012). Further, corporations must consider the imperative of transparency, as it has been found that a lack of disclosure in a social media campaign may damage the organization-public relationship and the overall credibility of the organization (Sweetser, 2010). Research has shown news media are receptive to the concept of corporate social responsibility and often choose to incorporate the content into newspapers and other media outlets (Zhang & Swanson, 2006). Thus, both the source and the media format offer the opportunity to present cues that can influence the perception of the corporate social responsibility program. By utilizing these approaches, CSR communications can advance the platform.

Corporations implementing CSR programs often seek to intensify the relationship with a key stakeholder audience. Decisions are made in real time to determine the words and images to articulate the CSR campaign in a way that attracts the audiences to the effort. In an examination of a utility company's corporate social responsibility efforts, research revealed how a corporation may demonstrate commitment to constituents though words and images, and then attempt to link those with behavioral relationships (Hall, 2006). This work indicates a positive correlation between the impact of corporate philanthropy and relationships, which may in turn influence the perceived credibility of the source. Marin and Ruiz (2007) found that corporate social responsibility programs enhance corporate identity attractiveness in a stronger way than they contribute to perceptions of corporate ability, thus showing the potential impact on the consumer-company context. In a practical sense then, consumers believe the company is more attractive with the presence of a CSR effort. The emotional connection becomes important. CSR activities directly influence corporate ability and that a positive affective component is necessary to solidify that relationship (Marin & Ruiz, 2007). This is important to the analysis of source and media format on perceived credibility because these two factors directly influence the formulation of the consumer-company relationship and the positive or negative perception of the relationship. For the public relations practitioner, this means the continued question to find the right medium and source for the information.

In addition to the consumer's role in attribution and the amount of elaboration that they put forth, it has been found that when a company is well known to a consumer, a CSR strategy is more effective in influencing both corporate consumer ability and corporate social responsibility associations, which in turn lead to company and product evaluations (Kim, 2011). Consumers may tend to assume a company is good at making reliable products when they associate the company with a strong corporate social responsibility program, thus transferring the effects of the CSR campaign into perceptions that will ultimately benefit the corporation. However, the methods a company chooses to communicate this information remain a vexing challenge as it searches for the appropriate source and media format. Further, this landscape unearths the question about the role of the public relations professional. In addition, there may be negative perceptions of corporate social responsibility if it is linked to a publicity exercise or self-promotion. Some assert a model of distributive leadership is needed in order to give communicators a role in CSR leadership that may dispel charges of self-promotion (Benn et al., 2010).

The advent of consumer-to-consumer online media environments, including social networks such as Facebook, Instagram, TikTok, and many others, has changed the landscape for corporate communication and altered the way information is created and disseminated by corporations, because individuals can now conduct word-of-mouth communication in a web-based environment. Corporations and individuals now have the opportunity to add "sentiment messages" that endorse a specific consumer social responsibility campaign. Public relations professionals have a vast toolbox for communication yet choosing the right media format and message becomes vitally important. For example, the news release is a common tool of the public relations industry used by corporations to relay relevant corporate happenings and engage in media relations. A news article is a media format that readers may believe has passed through an editorial filter, allowing for an objective, third-party analysis of the content and justification that it is in fact newsworthy. An advertisement is a paid media format that consumers may recognize as a message that is completely controlled by the corporation. With these factors in mind, the imperative remains that a corporation must use a credible source and appropriate media format to convey aspects of the company's corporate social responsibility program that will in turn allow the company to harvest desired benefits. With the global pandemic, businesses found themselves communicating across the miles to employees and consumers who were now gaining information through mobile devices and computers at a dizzying pace.

Choosing the Right Media Format or Marketing Mix

Corporations that choose to undertake a CSR program consider the source, the media format, and the message (Coombs & Holladay, 2012). Further, with co-creation of media content, online key influencers have emerged as credible sources. We can contemplate the advent of YouTube celebrities, TikTokkers, and the like who address myriad topics and have gained the endorsement of thousands of followers. For example, both a corporation and an individual may transmit CSR information in the form of a news release, article, or advertisement via social media. In practice, consider if your social media friend endorses a corporate social responsibility campaign, are you more likely to accept the campaign's legitimacy? Dou et al. (2012) have indicated that the visible source plays a role in influencing the credibility judgment. The content class may also serve as a cue for cognitive processing of information (Hallahan, 1999). A message that originates from a corporation versus one that originates with a consumer may have differences in stimulating source credibility. This is particularly interesting as the sender chooses to transmit various media formats including a news release, article, or advertisement. In persuasive communication, research suggests that the credibility of information sources plays a vital role in credibility measurements (Dou et al., 2012). The chosen media format influences a receiver's perception of information in a corporate social responsibility campaign (Kiousis et al., 2011). Online trust can be enhanced through social cue design in online environments (Metzger, 2007). So, with these various forces at work, the corporation must carefully choose key influencers who can carry the message to broader audiences in a credible way.

Information Credibility Impact for Public Relations Professionals

Public relations professionals seeking to communicate with credible information have rapidly learned to adapt to the pandemic environment. When examining the marketing mix, therefore, corporations can place a higher priority on the public relations program and a lower priority on the paid advertising found in marketing departments. Further, management should include public relations professionals in the CSR decision-making process. For the public relations professional, in a corporate social responsibility effort, the public relations program should transmit content to consumers, which can in turn be shared with others, allowing for viral communication. In addition, the public relations professional continues to provide information to the company's board of directors, management team, and other decision-makers who are devising and implementing corporate social responsibility programs.

With various types of media formats available to corporations to convey the specific aspects of the corporate social responsibility campaign, it seems relevant therefore to once again get into the mind of the recipient to see how they receive and interpret the data. For example, academic research has shown that attributions play a key role in determining the extent to which consumers interact with user-generated content (Dunn & Harness, 2018). For example, if the recipient views the communication as self-promotion, it may be discarded as "greenwashing," turning the reader off to the intended message and disenfranchising the company. Yet with the prevalence of social media, we now observe a rich environment of collaboration between the company and the key stakeholders, allowing for the formation of a consumer-company bond (Uzunoğlu et al., 2017). With this bond, the company has the opportunity to further spread the "news" of a corporate social responsibility initiative, enlisting participants and fulfilling the mission of the campaign. In particular, consumers actually value the transparency of communicating online and the corporate social responsibility communication can enhance the consumer's level of admiration of the company and the brand (Gupta, Nawaz, Alfalah, et al.). Corporate social responsibility programs have been shown to generate a positive and significant effect on brand performance (Hesari & Shadiardehaei, 2021). With all of this evidence then, it becomes apparent that a company undertaking a corporate social responsibility program must therefore communicate effectively with multiple stakeholders to form the appropriate bond. This bond, however, is delicate and can be called into question if the CSR effort is viewed as self-serving.

So with the benefit of transparency, the bond of trust can emerge between the corporation and stakeholders. It should be noted that while online media may increase awareness, "legacy" types of communication such as newspapers, television, radio and interpersonal communication have been shown to further facilitate engagement and participation in corporate social responsibility efforts (Lee et al., 2019). When companies can harness the value of word-of-mouth communication, it can yield dividends for the CSR campaign. For example, public relations professionals may elect to use key influencers online to fuel the spread of the corporate social responsibility campaign by leveraging the positive cues and social power of the influencer (Kim & Xu, 2019). When engaged in dialogic communication with key stakeholders, the company can inform others about the CSR program and promote information diffusion and endorsement of specific activities (Araujo & Kollat, 2018).

As companies struggle to cope with the global pandemic, we observe renewed practical applications for corporate social responsibility. From Dove's "Health Hero" campaign to the cash donations by corporations, the intersection of private enterprise and public health is even more apparent. The connections between audiences and corporations become a more dynamic field, fueled by communication that takes many forms, both online and offline. Businesses with strategic corporate social responsibility programs can harvest vast benefits including increased brand loyalty, purchase intention, and connection to the brand. Successful public relations professionals choose the right media formats and channels for communication.

TIPS FOR COMMUNICATING ONLINE ABOUT CORPORATE SOCIAL RESPONSIBILITY

1. Perform research about the media consumption habits of key stakeholders
2. Plan the communication channels
3. Execute in a timely, consistent fashion
4. Allow for dialogic dimensions and co-creation with key stakeholders
5. Establish feedback loops with key stakeholders
6. Retool the communication programs by examining channels
7. Allow time for a concerted communication effort

COMMUNICATION THAT LEADS TO PARTICIPATION

Through effective communication, the corporate communicator can develop meaningful relationships with stakeholders. However, the pitfalls of claims of "self-promotion," untimely messages, or "off-target" communications indicate ongoing threats in the formulation of a CSR stakeholder ecosystem.

- Research first, communicate second: Savvy communicators avoid a common mistake: communicating without the benefit of research. To analyze this equation, consider the following: For whom is the program? What is the social, political, or economic situation that they are facing? How will this corporate program address this issue? How is this CSR program different from others that exist?
- Understand the stakeholders (and how they prefer to receive information): By understanding the habits and attitudes of CSR stakeholders, you will glean valuable information about how to communicate with them, when to communicate with them, and what messages will mean the most for them. For example, a cause marketing program benefitting cancer research has an immediate group of stakeholders, including patients, hospital staff, physicians, and families. However, don't forget that each of these audiences consumes media in a different way. To effectively communicate with them, we must first understand, through research, their communication habits.

- Articulate what matters: Once the CSR campaign is established and operating in the marketplace, the temptation to report ancillary fun facts or contiguous comments becomes tempting. Always consider the strategic message and how to effectively communicate that message. By reporting specific outcomes of the effort, the impact may be "shown" and not simply "told." Further, consider first-person stories and testimonials from the campaign itself. By attaching faces to a campaign, the CSR moves from beyond a corporate initiative to a human one.
- Avoid self-serving language while still emphasizing corporate participation: Corporations that undertake CSR initiatives deserve an opportunity to convey their roles in the specific campaign. Company spokespersons, trained in the key messages of the campaign, should actively articulate various aspects in the program across all media outlets. While some critics chastise businesses for "self-serving" promotion, language designed to focus on the CSR program outcomes and the beneficiaries can help to minimize this criticism.
- Manage your feedback: A mature CSR communications program will yield something even more valuable than the results themselves. A CSR program will enable the corporation to reach key stakeholders in a meaningful way and establish two-way communication information loops. Communicators must actively monitor this feedback and determine the best ways to return messages and facilitate meaningful dialogue.

The strategic creation of a CSR message must not be an "afterthought" in the executive decision-making process. By aligning the CSR program objectives with communication objectives, the foundation of an integrated communications program may be formulated. With appropriate budget, staff, and participation in the senior leadership of CSR decision-making, the individuals who craft the CSR message will dramatically contribute to the ultimate success for the CSR program.

Chapter 5

Social Media Engagement in a CSR Program

Social media's pervasiveness has led to a cacophony of referrals to products, social causes, and political candidates. Corporate social responsibility communication is not immune to the dialogic dimensions of communication found in the social media sphere. Corporations have jumped on the CSR bandwagon to effectively utilize all aspects of paid, earned, shared, and "owned" media to carry the corporate social responsibility messages beyond the walls of their organization to the constituencies where the program can make a difference. Today, citizens communicate across the miles through social media channels, taking corporate CSR messages and appropriating them as their own. Other social media mishaps may occur in the online sphere including hoaxes, deep fakes, and adapted videos that may obscure or obliterate original messages. Scholars continue to examine the intersection between social media and corporate social responsibility, suggesting that corporate social responsibility can lead to further resonance with key publics and reduce asymmetrical, one-way communication (Saxton, Gomez et al., 2019). CSR engagement enhances corporate image, which in turn can promote positive word of mouth (Vo et al., 2019). As corporations communicate back to audiences invested in corporate social responsibility, they are able to intensify stakeholder bonds, particular with stakeholders who possess their own loyal followers online (Saxton, Ren et al., 2021). Social media provides corporations and individuals a place to share information and form a community. Let's address how we gain information online and the trust attached to specific messages shared online.

EXAMINING SOURCE CREDIBILITY AND THE RELEVANCE TO SOCIAL MEDIA

During the Covid-19 pandemic, citizens shared information with each other about requirements for quarantine, masks, and immunizations. Yet the truthfulness and legitimacy of information is presented in a broad span. Information received from a friend may be considered with a higher level of trust. But is it accurate? Social scientific research has indicated that social cues influence source credibility, which in turn can persuade or disenfranchise an information recipient (Sternthal et al., 1978). The visible source influences the credibility and informs the receiver's judgment (Dou et al., 2012). Today, the social media environment provides a rich twenty-four/seven atmosphere to render source cues and proliferate electronic word of mouth. Coulter and Roggeveen (2012) found that electronic word of mouth relies on source expertise. In practice, corporate social responsibility information is often transferred with personal testimonials and opinions. Information receivers make instantaneous judgments about source credibility and their perceptions may be influenced by personal messages conveyed via social media. Professional communicators seeking to promote viral spread of information try to tap into this phenomenon with key messages, attractive graphics, and updated, timely information. In fact, research has shown that the credibility of a source can generate both affective and cognitive responses (Li, 2013). As corporations undertake the charge to convey corporate social responsibility information to key stakeholders, multiple questions regarding information credibility surround the situation. What is the best format to communicate in a way that will stimulate information credibility? Who is the best source of this information to promote conditions of information credibility? Communicators today have a wide range of media formats at their disposal to convey corporate social responsibility. Yet the tone of the communication is also important, as scholars have found that the public was more likely to generate word of mouth about a company or cause if the organization used a conversational tone when communicating with stakeholders (Oh & Ki, 2019).

The believability of specific media formats has been documented in scholarly literature for decades, showing various points of view regarding the credibility of one media format over another. Scholars have developed criteria and research scales to evaluate newspaper and television news credibility (Newhagen & Nass, 1989; Graziano & McGrath, 1986), looking into aspects of fairness, bias, telling the complete story, accuracy, invasion of privacy, advocacy for viewer's interest, concern with community's well-being, separation of fact and opinion, trustworthiness, advocacy for public interest, factual nature, and the existence of well-trained reporters. Today the availability of online information has led to the formation of new scales oriented to online content, including a scale by Flanagin and Metzger (2000) that tests the credibility of online information by examining its believability, accuracy, trustworthiness, bias, and completeness. Corporations continue to leverage both internal and external messages carried by chief executive officers to more broadly convey key corporate social responsibility program attributes via social media (Wang & Huang, 2018).

EVOLVING THE MEDIA RELATIONS PARADIGM

In the public relations field, the news media relations function has been a proven and long-standing discipline. Public relations practitioners develop a full array of media relations tools including news media kits, news releases, video news releases, fact sheets, media alerts, tip sheets, and social media plans. While media relations may provide one tactic for communications, companies must pursue other media options, according to scholars (Bhattacharya et al., 2011; Coombs & Holladay, 2012). Certainly, the availability of rich media formats and new channels for communication open up new universes for dialogue. Academic scholarship on various media formats has indicated that the differences in credibility may be based on the nature of the media themselves and how information is perceived about them, leading to different information-processing strategies (Newhagen & Nass, 1989). This is particularly relevant today with social media's role in mass media. Today, consumers may expose themselves to media sources and content that may be unreliable and they may do so repeatedly, influencing their beliefs of credibility. Thus, we may observe consumers using social media for corporate and product information despite a perceived absence of credibility. In a sense then, we observe the flattening of social communication as citizens share information with each other.

Research has indicated that enfranchising stakeholders into the corporate social responsibility process allows them to function as message carriers in the social media environment and promote viral forms of communication (Coombs & Holladay, 2012). Metzger (2007) has suggested that credibility assessments of online information include three phases including exposure, evaluation, and judgment. The use of persuasive messages with social media sentiment (a customized statement) may provide personal appeals to the receiver that in essence perform a "priming" or "framing" role for corporate social responsibility communication. Contemporary businesses seek to persuade stakeholders about the positive aspects of corporate social responsibility in an effort to enhance corporate and brand reputation (Diermeier, 2011). Scholars have issued a plea for businesses to use social media as a tool for corporate social branding (Kesavan et al., 2013). Two sources of corporate social responsibility information may be the corporation or another consumer. As they attach a supplemental message to the message, persuasive impacts may be measured by the "sentiment" exerted in a social media atmosphere. For example, the material could be viewed by the reader as credible or unreliable. This perception may be further influenced by the accompanying message that may endorse or erode the brand message conveyed via social media.

THE INFLUENCE OF SOURCE AND MEDIA FORMAT TO PROMOTE SOCIAL MEDIA ENGAGEMENT

Businesses seeking to convey information about a corporate social responsibility program want to use the most effective sources and media formats to catalyze social media engagement. In an era of dialogic communication, online media formats have opened the gates to consumer-to-consumer communication, allowing for a new environment of online word of mouth. Often housed within a social media platform such as Facebook, Tiktok, or myriad other social media, consumers now convey their thoughts, beliefs, and opinions to followers. This provides a new dimension for corporate communication, particularly related to corporate social responsibility. We now interact, share ideas, issue opinions, and offer approvals. Interactivity is at the center of dialogic communication. Choosing the most effective sources and formats to communicate may create advantageous conditions for corporations conveying CSR information. However, commanding the social media environment to systematically fuel word-of-mouth communication has been elusive for some corporations. Some organizations remain reticent to use new formats, while others rely on traditional channels. Social media provides opportunities for stakeholders to come forth in a two-way symmetrical communications position with the corporation, but the media format also allows for broadcasting of CSR messages to specific communities via posts, likes, and transmission of CSR content. Audiences that choose to engage in corporate social responsibility communication may be seeking their own reward, gaining a position of "thought leadership," or advancing their social standing among social media friends.

Scholars have examined the impact of word of mouth in both offline and online environments (Brown & Dacin, 1997; Feng & Papatla, 2011). Consumers are driven by the desire for social interaction, economic incentives, concern for other consumers, and the potential to enhance their own self-worth when they contemplate electronic word-of-mouthbehavior (Hennig-Thurau et al., 2004). Traditional word of mouth no longer takes place in a face-to-face format, but has instead been replaced by electronic word of mouth, what has been coined eWOM. Consumers and citizens use social media formats to testify to a product attribute, examine ethical behavior, or condemn a corporation for failed products or irresponsible social behavior. Worley (2007) has called the Internet a "great equalizer" in terms of relationship building. Further, in setting forth multiple categories of CSR discourse including discourse on organizational legitimacy, philanthropy responsibility, products and services responsibility, environmental responsibility, and responsibility to workers, Worley asserts that corporations must do so in an atmosphere of dialogic communication. Word of mouth is related to the concept of customer engagement, indicating customers' comprehensive behaviors directed toward a corporation. Researchers divided customer engagement into community engagement behaviors and transactional engagement behaviors. In an analysis of customer engagement in a Facebook brand community, it was found that customer behavioral engagement positively influences relationships. Engagement activities such as writing comments and reading messages positively influences relationship benefits (Gummerus et al., 2012). In a study of the use of a social network to signal trustworthiness of an unfamiliar e-vendor, Brengman and Karimov (2012) found that simply including a social media site in the online retailer's website the corporation successfully signaled aspects of "benevolence" and "integrity." Kaplan and Haenlein (2011) define electronic word of mouth as "viral marketing" that a corporation can use by "giving the right message to the right messengers in the right environment" (Kaplan & Haenlein, 2011, p. 253). The presence of viral marketing in corporate social responsibility allows consensus to assume positions of thought leadership.

TWO-WAY COMMUNICATION BETWEEN AUDIENCES AND ORGANIZATIONS

As consumers engage with corporations via mediated communication, scholars must examine how consumers talk to each other and how they "talk back" to the company. It has been found that online networks are a social proxy for individual identification (Brown et al., 2007). This means that corporations have the opportunity to leverage social media networks for engagement and advance word of mouth into electronic word of mouth regarding corporate social responsibility initiatives. Lopez and Sicilia (2013) found that information diffusion of new product information is enhanced when word-of-mouth activities occur before advertising. Other scholars have found that increased brand advertising can be associated with reduced online word of mouth for products, thus indicating that traditional advertising may not always be compatible with word-of-mouth approaches (Feng & Papatla, 2011). Today, corporations remain in an evolving process of understanding the most beneficial ways to use these media channels. New channels emerge, and thought leaders remain fluid, making the need for measurement and issue monitoring very important. Public relations practitioners seek to master various uses of paid, earned, shared, and owned media to make the most persuasive and engaging campaigns possible. In an analysis of corporate social responsibility websites of corporations, Capriotti and Moreno (2007) found that while corporations articulate CSR programs on websites, they often fail to promote interactivity. In an examination of corporate websites, a common communication medium used by corporate communicators, researchers found an absence of two-way reciprocal communication. Instead, many CSR corporate websites focused on "expositive information" rather than interactive resources. This phenomenon thus negates the formation of a communication loop that allows consumers to "talk back" to the corporation. Further, the absence of this channel may leave consumers seeking for other media distribution channels to transmit opinions about a corporate social responsibility campaign.

New communication techniques to leverage the communication power of social media outlets are being created by scholars across the globe. Scholarly findings indicate that Fortune 500 companies may strive to engage stakeholders in dialogue using media formats like Twitter, but fail to authentically create an atmosphere of two-way communication (Rybalko & Seltzer, 2010). However, companies can be successful at creating relationships with consumers and enhance the brand by using interactive communication techniques such as online blogs, if the company believes in customer empowerment (Singh et al., 2008). Jenkins (2006) has written about the advent of a convergence culture that puts the power of social media engagement in the hands of every smart phone user and laptop cruiser. Media convergence is more than simply a technology shift. Convergence alters the relationship between existing technologies, industries, markets, genres, and audiences. Convergence alters the logic by which media industries operate and by which media consumers process news and entertainment. Keep this in mind: Convergence refers to a process, not an end-point. Convergence involves both a change in the way that media produces and a change in the way media is consumed (Jenkins, 2006, pp. 15–16). Argenti (2009) points to the fact that technology has fueled the phenomenon of corporations engaging stakeholders in two-way conversations about corporate social responsibility. Contemporary consumers use media in a way to gratify their own self interests.

Consumers today seek information about green initiatives and corporate philanthropy, allowing corporations to use a multitude of communication channels including social media to convey messages and engage an array of stakeholders. Argenti (2006) calls the needs for CSR "immeasurable" and states that the risks of not doing so are "toxic." While Grunig and Grunig

(1992) have posited multiple models of public relations, the press-agentry model applies to CSR information research, as does Grunig and Grunig's model regarding two-way symmetrical communication. The advent of digital media denotes a new era of communication that suggests a new level of efficiency for dialogic, two-way symmetrical communication. Advocates for two-way symmetrical communication have gone so far to say that different "stakes" condition different dialogic types, and thus businesses must link the stakes to specific dialogue forms and scripts (Johansen & Nielsen, 2011). For example, a consumer stakeholder has the interest/stake of quality, thus requiring a dialogue form of networking and a dialogue rich with experience and engagement. The investor stakeholder has the stake of a financial return and requires the dialogue form of mutual briefing and a dialogue script of balancing and ensuring (Johansen & Nielsen, 2011). Despite criticism of the two-way symmetrical model, L'Etang (1994) states that the model may be employed by the corporation if it truly recognizes the issues brought forth by stakeholders and can balance those against pure self-interest. L'Etang argues that corporate social responsibility is a potential example of symmetrical public relations but can be recategorized as publicity or public information if it is communicated to a third party. As consumers and corporations enter into this new dialogic era, the role of the public relations professional continues to evolve as the professionals devise and carry the social media messages.

The Grunig symmetrical model has been used as a foundation to study corporate social responsibility communications. Morsing and Schultz (2006) unite stakeholder theory with the Grunig models and then pose three models for CSR communication: stakeholder information strategy, analogous to the Grunig model of publicity; stakeholder response strategy for two-way asymmetrical sensemaking and sensegiving; and stakeholder involvement strategy providing consideration for two-way symmetrical sensemaking and sensegiving. This approach concludes that companies will get the most benefit from facilitating "co-creation" of content. The two-way symmetrical model allows for communication of a message to a public/receiver who then transmits a message back to the sender that results in some form of adaptation or meaningful change. The two-way symmetrical viewpoint is a systems-based model that presumes the corporation will listen to and subscribe to changes suggested by the stakeholders. Yet this is only one part of social media engagement. The consumer has the opportunity as a content creator to pass along information of relevance to a specific community.

With this evidence, scholars continue to suggest a changing role for the contemporary public relations professional, moving away from a traditional press agentry role to one characterized by community building and establishment of two-way communication loops. Further insights regarding the role of the public relations professional may be gleaned through the work of Kruckeberg et al. (2006), who address the role and ethics of community building for consumer products and services. They point to facets of a consumer community such as a continuing presence, belief of the community in the merits of the service or product, a shared culture revolving around the service or product, and a community characterized by dynamism and normative behavior in relation to the product or service. With this in mind, the public relations professional must play an integral role in consumer community development. Academic research and practical observations of social media habits reveal that the platform provides a venue for dialogic communication regarding corporate social responsibility, allowing for intensified customer engagement and relationship building.

DIALOGIC PRINCIPLES AT WORK IN SOCIAL MEDIA

As corporations form relationships with consumers in the delicate stakeholder relationship, social media may serve as a fertile channel for communication. Kent and Taylor (1998) have suggested principles of dialogic communication that fuel relationships, promote communication, and potentially foster desired behaviors in the social media sphere. Yet that evolution of electronic word of mouth suggests an emerging and more advanced role for the consumer (Hennig-Thurau et al., 2004). A consumer who receives CSR information online will likely make judgments regarding the corporation or the consumer who transmitted the information. In turn, the receiver will make choices on whether to retransmit information or not based on the source credibility. For example, the consumer may experience a higher level of comfort participating in two-way dialogue with another consumer about a CSR program, rather than communicating with a corporation. Further, following CSR online exposure, an advocacy role may be exercised as the consumer exerts behaviors such as "likes," "shares," or "posts" in an online media environment. Social media environments serve as channels of communication for both consumers and corporations. Corporations may use social media outlets to convey corporate messages while consumers come to social media environments to fulfill needs (Gummerus et al., 2012). Some researchers have distinguished behaviors between "community engagement" and "transactional" behaviors. The prompting of social media engagement may be influenced by the information source of the media format used to convey the information. The level of engagement may be influenced by the connection between the consumer and corporation, or alternatively the consumer and another consumer. This phenomenon is examinedby Kruckeberg et al. (2006), who address the notion of a shared culture that revolves around a product or service. This concept may be applied to corporate social responsibility information. The type of media format adds a second dynamic to the equation as the receiver may discern aspects of source credibility and information credibility. For example, a consumer may be more likely to "post" information from a corporation if they feel a strong community connection and that information is presented in a credible way by using a media format such as an advertisement, article, or news release. In light of the myriad media content choices, the media consumer performs a more active role, generating content and communicating directly with the corporation. We can now observe one-to-one communication on a broader scale, allowing relationships to form.

MEDIA CONSUMERS AS CONTENT PRODUCERS

Research suggests a new atmosphere of convergence is flooding the corporate marketplace, changing the ecosystem of media consumption and media production (Jenkins, 2006). The willingness of a consumer to engage with a corporation or another individual when presented with corporate social responsibility information may be influenced by a secondary "appeal" by the corporation or by the information. As information spreads virally via social media, personal endorsements and testimonials may attempt to persuade the individual to engage with the content by liking, sharing, or posting the information. In the social media sphere, engagement can intensify as dialogic communication occurs. This level of engagement may further propel electronic word of mouth (Gummerus et al., 2012). As Worley (2007) indicated, corporate social responsibility discourse must include multiple facets such as legitimacy and philanthropy, and must be conveyed through dialogic communication. By establishing atmospheres for dialogue, companies can advance corporate communication platforms. While corporations may gravitate to brand advertising as a way to communicate, this tactic may reduce word of mouth (Feng & Papatla, 2011). Further, the role of the consumer as a co-creator of content should not be discounted. Therefore, investigation is required to determine the interaction of source, media format, and sentiment in the communication of corporate social responsibility programs.

When it comes to relaying content, consumers can choose to like, share, or post graphics, videos, news releases, and advertisements. For managerial purposes, this suggests the use of a viable public relations program that is designed to generate news releases and conduct news media relations. These media relations activities become a pivotal aspect of a corporate social responsibility campaign, because the content can be disseminated via social media and virally shared. It should also be noted there is a compelling role for the public relations professional in CSR planning, as has been advocated by Freitag (2005). Further arguments for the active role of the public relations professional have been advocated by Coombs and Holladay (2009) and Freitag (2005). With the interaction between corporate social responsibility campaigns and social, economic, and political issues, citizens may actively seek CSR information and interpret the data in a favorable way.

THE ENGAGED CORPORATE SOCIAL RESPONSIBILITY AUDIENCE AS ACTIVISTS AND THOUGHT LEADERS

Yet, while a corporation may be driven to establish source credibility for profit motives, brand building, or advancement of the CSR program, consumers may be driven by a different motive. It has been indicated that consumers fulfill their own desires through electronic word-of-mouth activities (Hennig-Thurrau et al., 2004), and the sentiment messages employed by this research study provide a new avenue for communication that can match desires for promoting their own self-worth. When communicating to various audiences, the company may successfully meet what has been called the "consumer demand for virtue" by Diermeier (2011). Further, these sentiment messages may be a way to further solidify corporate trust in a corporate social responsibility program, which has already been deemed as a credible way for a corporation to boost trust (Pivato et al., 2008).

When companies insert messages directing viewers to content and convey "person-to-person" aspects of communication, they can endorse specific ideas, products, and corporate social responsibility programs. Thus, the company spokesperson not only can leverage the corporate authoritativeness, but may also experience advanced personal credibility. This may occur when an individual representative (spokesperson) relays the message as a consumer, not just as a corporate spokesperson. Consumers seeking to gain recognition as a credible source with "character" should make an extra effort to include personal sentiment messages when transmitting information about a corporate social responsibility program. By integrating person-to-person messages, the consumer thus energizes the word of mouth and positions himself or herself as an individual with "character," one who may be trusted to convey useful and reliable information. This activity typifies aspects of stakeholder engagement that have been called for by Coombs and Holladay (2012) and Korschun and Du (2013). Co-creation of content with the corporation can be effective and dialogic principles (Kent & Taylor, 2002) applied in CSR communication situations. The active participation of the consumer demonstrates the act of co-creation that generates valuable dialogue networks (Korschun & Du, 2013). Consumers in the contemporary media atmosphere can take on an active role of content creation.

IMPLICATIONS FOR CORPORATE COMMUNICATION IN THE SOCIAL MEDIA SPHERE

The advent of new social media channels has marked a new era of dialogic communication that mandates advanced mastery for corporations seeking to articulate corporate social responsibility information. As we consider the online sphere and social media, we can do so within the context of building a community. The corporation maintains a corporate persona that directly communicates with various key publics to advance the specific platform, which may include green activities, cause promotion, or cause marketing initiatives. This chapter explored the importance of a credible source to carry the corporate social responsibility message across multiple social media channels. By looking at the role of the public relations professional, the chief executive officer, and the audience in creating and proliferating content, we have found that corporate social responsibility activities conceived with a strategic purpose can enhance the corporation's reputation and bind myriad key stakeholders to the organization.

Chapter 6

Promoting Purchase Intention through Corporate Social Responsibility Communication

Corporations often utilize corporate social responsibility programs as a technique to further bind consumers to the company in an effort to further generate sales. Whether we examine consumer products, manufactured goods, or retail establishments, corporate social responsibility programs hum through sales and brand management. In fact, research has shown that high-tech companies seeking to maximize sales should contemplate CSR practices in the environmental domain (Tian et al., 2020). As corporations utilize corporate social responsibility programs to gain further trust with key publics, the businesses emerge with a greater prowess to sell products uniquely positioned for the consumers who sympathize with corporate social responsibility causes. Customers in tune with corporate social responsibility programs seem willing to support the programs by purchasing goods and services. For businesses, the program can help to engender trust with key publics, delivering short-term and long-term rewards. This activity gives rise to new "green" products and cause-oriented marketing. The connection between CSR activities and purchase intention is clear. Academic research has shown that active CSR campaigns promote consumers' purchase intention, and a global mindset also advanced purchase intention (Liu et al., 2018). The desire for businesses to promote top-line growth and positive bottom-line impact through corporate social responsibility programs remains a common objective (Elkington, 1997). Corporations are undertaking CSR programs to fulfill shareholder obligations in a multitude of ways. Businesses are able to fulfill fiduciary responsibilities and meet obligations to engage in society in an ethical manner. Stimulating the act of purchase requires the formation of trust, and active corporate social responsibility programs harmonize with the trust-building agenda. Through well-crafted efforts, corporate social responsibility can boost trust and, in turn, promote purchase intention, allowing the corporation to simultaneously meet corporate objectives and deliver meaningful, socially oriented programs for society at large. It is worth noting that the willingness for consumers to pay more for social features and the impact of ethics on purchasing behavior also influence research involving corporate communication and corporate social responsibility. Observers of corporate social responsibility note that the ability to strategically define and auspiciously implement corporate social responsibility programs can lead to significant results.

Scholars have examined this phenomenon, finding significant evidence that well-planned and executed corporate social responsibility can deliver business results. It has been found that consumers who identify with CSR activities in social media, develop a more intensive identification with the brand and social media engagement, which subsequently contributes to purchase intention activities (Chu & Chen, 2019). It has also been shown that corporate social responsibility actions of a bank will actually contribute to the likelihood that consumers will purchase from the bank and lead to admiration of the corporation (Gupta et al., 2021). Today, some consumers actively seek out ethical firms to purchase from, and support brands that are willing to engage in corporate social responsibility programs. Consumers look for and endorse products that resonate with their core value systems. Ethical features of a product have a substantial impact on the purchase intentions of consumers (Auger et al., 2003). This means that consumers may actively search for a product that utilizes an ethical supply chain, or offers a portion of proceeds to a nonprofit organization. Further, researchers underscore the importance of communication in bridging the CSR program and purchasing intention. Scholars have also suggested that corporations can increase consumer engagement in their corporate social responsibility programs through education-oriented communication that articulates and explains corporate sponsorship and activity with public organizations (Lee & Yoon, 2018). Therefore, it is vital for marketing communications efforts to effectively unite the product with the ethics so that consumers can understand the philanthropic dimensions, and at times be willing to serve as a brand ambassador, influencing others to make a corresponding purchase. In fact, the emergence of corporate social responsibility programs has given rise to another phenomenon that consumers may be willing to spend even more cash than usual to invest in an ethical firm. The ethicality of a firm's behavior is an important consideration during the purchasing decision, and consumers will reward ethical behavior by paying higher prices (Creyer & Ross, 1996). With this in mind, it becomes imperative that corporations actively use various modes of communication to speak with consumers in a way to explain the value proposition of the corporate social responsibility products and services. Despite all of this, some consumers may simply not value CSR, but rather seek the lowest prices. It should be noted these customers may not be the loyal brand advocates. Therefore, to further gain trust with brand advocates savvy marketers will look for ways to effectively communicate, breathe through the clutter, and convey ethical information in a favorable way.

Consistent with the complexity of purchasing decisions as a whole, the relationship between corporate social responsibility and purchasing contains multiple influences and a variety of factors. Sen and Bhattacharya (2001) have found that the relationship between corporate social responsibility and the subsequent influence on consumer purchase intention is a complex one. CSR can affect consumers' intentions to purchase products both directly and indirectly. Under certain CSR domains like employee working conditions, consumers with CSR-related belief systems can be influenced by the CSR activities. For example, consumers must be made to feel that the corporate social responsibility program does not detract from the company's ability to produce quality products (Sen & Bhattacharya, 2001). In other words, while some consumers are ethical and "civic minded," they still want to purchase products of quality. Brown and Dacin (1997) examined the influences of corporate ability (CA) and corporate social responsibility (CSR), categorizing them both as corporate associations that may influence perceptions and consumer responses. They found that while CSR associations may exert influence on product evaluations, a company's corporate ability evaluation metric may have a greater impact. Thus, a reputation based on the company's ability carries greater power than a reputation for social responsibility (Brown & Dacin, 1997). For public relations professionals, this finding suggests that communication must operate with multiple strategic objectives—to communicate the capability and value of the company and also indicate that the company can legitimately exercise ethical behavior through corporate social responsibility programs. The research component of CSR activities is vital at this stage, employing audience research that would identify stakeholders and their characteristics, lifestyle choices, and communication preferences. Further, consumers with a global orientation often embrace CSR purchasing behaviors more readily (Liu et al., 2018). Customers want proven products that are going to work and are affordable. If these same products support an enlightened, philanthropic cause, that is even more meaningful for the buyer.

CHARACTERISTICS OF CORPORATE SOCIAL RESPONSIBILITY PURCHASING BEHAVIOR

A number of commonalities may be found among consumers who exhibit eco-purchasing behavior. For example, they may be willing to engage in the ethical stance of the company, pay more for ethically sourced goods and services, and perform the role of a brand ambassador. Corporate identity and corporate reputation management play a vital role in the administration of CSR programs. Marketing researchers focus on financial outcomes of corporate social responsibility programs while public relations researchers concentrate on less tangible variables such as goodwill and corporate relationships (David et al., 2005). To bridge the gap between the two disciplines, academic researchers have suggested the formation of a new definition of corporate identity, one that includes both dimensions of corporate expertise and corporate social responsibility, and propose a model of corporate identity that encompasses both an exchange dimension, based on utility, and a citizenship dimension, characterized by social values. This approach yields a dual process model that serves as the foundation of their research, which unites a path between CSR values and purchase intention (David et al., 2005). A connection between brand familiarity and CSR behaviors may also have a significant effect on purchase intention. With this in mind, we can better understand the enlightened customer who wants a useful product and one that will exhibit good citizenship.

CONSUMER ENGAGEMENT WITH CORPORATE SOCIAL RESPONSIBILITY PROGRAMS

To entice consumers to engage with the brand and promote purchase intention, corporations must achieve a higher level of consumer engagement. Yet the challenge to create a community of CSR-friendly users remains. To succeed, the programs must harmonize with the stakeholder's value system to instill trust and promote action, which may take the form of various communications. In the exploration of the connection between corporate social responsibility and purchase intention, it is important to examine the harmony of the specific CSR campaign with the beliefs of the consumer. David et al. (2005) found both corporate expertise and corporate social values may serve as significant predictors of purchase intention, as evidenced by a study of four large corporations: Microsoft, Nike, Philip Morris, and Wendy's. So we may ponder why the corporate social value influences the specific attitudes and purchase intention of the consumers. In an analysis of how and why corporate social responsibility activity leads individual stakeholders to produce company-favoring outcomes, Bhattacharya et al. (2009) found that CSR provides stakeholders with numerous types of benefits. They go further to establish a stakeholder-centric model for understanding CSR that reveals ways stakeholders respond to CSR initiatives, based on how they derive personal benefits from the effort and how the stakeholder-company relationship is influenced by the type of benefits accrued. These researchers found the quality of the resulting stakeholder-company relationship from a CSR program relates to the type of benefits harvested by the stakeholder.

With this in mind, the question then becomes, how do consumers access corporate social responsibility information? Bhattacharya et al. (2009) encourage scholars and practitioners to probe the process through which stakeholders assess CSR initiatives, suggesting that further study is required to analyze the effect of various sources and media formats in generating favorable conditions for CSR evaluation, which in turn can lead to brand awareness, purchase intention, and social media engagement. In addition to the stakeholder "gain" that can occur in a CSR relationship, the aspect of trust plays a part in catalyzing future actions of consumers, most notably purchase intention. Pivato et al. (2008) examined the organic food industry and found that corporate social performance can influence consumer trust, which in turn influences consumers' subsequent actions. They found that CSR generates trust and this trust translates into brand loyalty and the intention to purchase products (Pivato et al., 2008). The preexisting value system of the consumer also plays a factor in the engendering of trust and subsequent purchase intention. Therefore, what we believe and corresponding values influence our purchasing behaviors. It has also been found that personal values of consumers translate into buying decisions. In a study of consumer's motivational orientation to promotion versus prevention in green advertising appeals, Hsuan-Hsuan (2012) found that prevention-focused participants were more strongly persuaded when "product-related" appeals emphasize green rather than nongreen attributes. Another study found that product preference was enhanced by "green" rather than nongreen appeals (Ku et al., 2012). In an analysis of fair trade consumption, Doran (2009) found a correlation between personal values and the willingness to support fair trade companies that protect integrity in a corporate supply chain so as not to take advantage of producers.

In a study analyzing whether a company's social responsibility record matters to consumers and if they are willing to pay higher prices for products from socially responsible companies, Mohr and Webb (2005) found that when consumers receive information that they trust about the company's level of social responsibility, it affects how they evaluate the company and influences the purchasing intention. The study also found that a low price did not appear to compensate for low levels of social responsibility (Mohr & Webb, 2005). In an atmosphere of trust, it is understood that a highly involved individual who agrees with the message will interpret it more positively than others (Upadhye et al., 2019). This notion further endorses the need for "communities" around companies, products, and services. Therefore, in this quest for trust, how corporations choose to communicate corporate social responsibility, by designating a source and specifying a media format, will ultimately impact purchase intention. Research suggests that purchase intention can be influenced if corporate ethical behavior can be properly communicated (Auger et al., 2003). The need to communicate remains vital to influencing purchasing intention, and the addition of CSR content can have a positive effect on building trust and changing attitudes.

In an attempt to secure relationships with key publics, corporations and marketing executives struggle to find the right source and format for conveying corporate social responsibility information. Some have called for the use of traditional public relations content as a way to build relationships with consumers, underscoring the publicity model of public relations (Grunig & Grunig, 1992), while others have asserted that the stakeholder must be presented with content in a media format that naturally fosters trust between the individual and the organization (Pivato et al., 2008). Corporations attempt to persuade consumers to purchase products and convey aspects of the corporate reputation by utilizing multiple media formats (Diermeier, 2011). The challenge in the CSR environment becomes a situation of communicating to stakeholders in a medium they can use and carry that message in a way that will resonate. Consumers may advocate for certain companies based on their preferences and value systems (Giacalone et al., 2005) and subsequently relay information contained in media formats to other consumers using social media. Corporations and consumers both have a multitude of communication choices available to them to convey corporate social responsibility information. As they make decisions regarding which media format to utilize, the outcomes for resulting purchase intention may vary.

As stated above, the aspect of trust remains an integral factor in the purchase intention equation (Pivato et al., 2008). Further, research has shown that a consumer must experience an association between their own personal values and a company with a corporate social responsibility campaign (Doran, 2009). This level of confidence may be influenced by the source of the communication and the accompanying sentiment that endorses the activity. To illustrate this phenomenon, consumers may embrace the credibility of a corporate source for corporate social responsibility information, or they could view it as self-serving as they attempt to attribute the reason why a corporation undertakes a CSR activity (Ellen et al., 2006). A detailed note of endorsement from the corporation could exacerbate the positive or negative aspects contributing to purchase intention. Consumers may view a fellow consumer as a trusted advisor and may be persuaded to purchase by a personal message, or similar to the corporate situation defined above, they may dislike the message and thus curtail purchasing, even based on the advice of a friend.

CREATING CSR STAKEHOLDER TRUST TO PROMOTE PURCHASE INTENTION

Contemporary marketers attempt to devise the most meaningful corporate social responsibility programs that may deliver bottom-line results. Research suggests that consumers may even pay higher prices for products from socially responsible companies (Mohr & Webb, 2005). To build the required trust, corporations must devise and implement appropriate communication strategies that consider the information source, media format, and use of persuasive social media techniques. Beyond the somewhat intangible "bond," it is the subsequent action that consumers take to purchase products that may define success for a CSR program. The actions that consumers exert to inform others about a corporate social responsibility campaign and to encourage others to join in "community" demonstrate the harmony of the consumer with the corporate social responsibility effort. Researchers have long identified the positive results of co-creation of content with consumers, further intensifying the bond of trust and confidence in decision-making. For example, Morsing and Schultz (2006) advocated for CSR co-creation between a corporation and its consumers. Starck and Kruckeberg (2001) discussed community formation for corporations, and Coulter and Roggeveen (2012) addressed social media engagement. Public relations programs have been known to promote purchase intension (Pirsch et al., 2007), and David et al. (2005) indicated that corporate social values, such as those found in CSR programs, represent predictors of purchase intention. The active communication of corporate social responsibility programs with credible communications gives the business a solid trust-building platform. Companies that maintain an active corporate social responsibility campaign gain what Kim (2011) has called "synergistic effects" of corporate ability, both for product quality and corporate reputation, as evidenced by the consumer relay of information. In essence, the consumers view the company and the specific products more favorably.

Social media presents a cacophony of information regarding corporate social responsibility (CSR). Some messages arrive on the consumer's device sent by the corporation, while others appear after transmitted by peers. While the messages can include transmission of a news release, article, or advertisement, questions remain regarding the effectiveness of various media in promoting consumer engagement. Lastly, while some sources provide sentiment messages to persuade eco-purchasing involvement, others simply retransmit or repost information. The concept of CSR has evolved in marketing and management literature as corporations struggle to devise the most effective techniques to convey aspects of the CSR effort and ultimately stimulate eco-purchasing involvement. Corporations undertake CSR initiatives for a multitude of reasons including forming relationships with stakeholders and enhancing profitability through sales. CSR remains an evolving paradigm with various definitions, yet many scholars rely on the Carroll (1979) definition, articulating CSR as a company's legal, ethical, environmental, and philanthropic responsibilities. The need to communicate effectively and persuasively remains an imperative for corporations seeking to stimulate eco-purchasing involvement. Multiple streams of literature provide background as appropriate sources and formats to convey CSR information are investigated. In particular, scholarship on the green purchase behaviors and the emerging role of the consumer in electronic word of mouth via social media are relevant, because without marketplace awareness and acceptance the program will falter. Marketing communications tools often play a vital role in articulating CSR information and these tools can help the company create a more socially responsible image (Jahdi & Acikdilli, 2009). Global corporations considered "green" may likely use social media to convey corporate communication information (Reilly & Hynan, 2014). The financial benefits to the corporation seem apparent and justifiably investigated. Businesses may use CSR to promote loyalty among consumers by leveraging the consumer's favorable identification with the company (Marin et al., 2009). Corporations can benefit from higher revenue with green products in the marketing mix because the company experiences gains in product-market performance (Leonidou et al., 2013). CSR communication, often found in an active public relations program, can drive market value by enhancing customer satisfaction and generating stakeholder value (Luo & Bhattacharya, 2006).

The Consumer's Role in Eco-Purchasing Behavior and CSR Communication

Yet the consumer's role in communication and the migration from CSR awareness to activism, articulated by information sharing and green product purchasing, presents a complex condition. The notion of pro-environmental behavior has been articulated as "pro-environmental consciousness," comprising knowledge, values, attitudes, and emotional involvement (Kollmuss & Agyeman, 2002). By analyzing buying patterns and learning more about the motivations, insights may be gleaned about the consumer's role in co-creation of CSR content. The consumer who chooses to engage in environmental purchasing may be influenced by multiple motivations, including social pressures and the desire to escalate in status. For example, an individual may leverage corporate social responsibility engagement to become a thought leader online. These desires, fulfilled through eco-purchasing involvement, may further contribute to the consumer's willingness to share information with a corresponding peer set via social media, and thus actively promote consumer-to-consumer communication about CSR activities. The impact on communication is evident as field experiments reveal that opinion leadership increases the indirect impact of mass communication messages (Batanic & Appel, 2013). By unlocking the connection between communication and persuasion, and the connection between personal desires and the intended actions, savvy communicators can master the trust dynamic to promote purchase intentions among consumers in tune with corporate social responsibility programs.

To unlock this puzzle, the profile of the environmentally sensitive buyer must be understood. Overall, based on a specific value system, they seek out information and often pay more for products, driven by their willingness to engage in an environmentally conscious CSR program. Research has shown significant interactions between personal values and fair trade consumption (Doran, 2009), further suggesting that communication must appeal to value systems. Environmentally concerned consumers ultimately show a greater interest in obtaining information about green initiatives and are more likely to associate that information with using the products (Bamberg, 2003). Individuals may gravitate to a company with a healthy CSR program because these philanthropic efforts resonate with the person's identity (Marin et al., 2006). Consumers who migrate to environmental purchasing habits can also exhibit behaviors that defy conventional logic, as they may pay more for an ethically conscious company's products (Creyer & Ross, 1996) and psychologically overcome purchasing risk by believing the conscious company offers greater value (Kwok et al., 2015). The willingness of consumers to pay is the strongest predictor of green purchasing behavior, followed by personal norms (Moser, 2015). To analyze how the environmental purchasing decisions can be influenced by various sources and media formats, it is important to recognize the underlying social needs that consumers satisfy through environmental purchasing. A win-win situation emerges as we examine the benefits to consumers and to the corporations. Consumers can derive value from CSR through emotional, social, and functional dimensions (Green & Peloza, 2011). Corporations ultimately benefit from creation of a green image that reveals a core competency in product innovation and processes (Chen, 2008), and bolsters brand equity from green brand image and green trust (Chen, 2010). The nexus between the brand image and the purchasing behavior remains apparent, yet social and economic pressures are also worth noting. While environmental concern remains important in the "green" purchase decision, social influence is also a factor (Tan et al., 2014). In an environmental buying decision, the social reference group influences individual cooperation by emphasizing social gain (Gupta & Ogden, 2009). Consumers inclined to purchase environmentally favorable products maintain a set of beliefs about their peer set, who may be exerting similar buying behavior, and thus can reinforce common belief systems through active communication. Buyers often equate going green with status and can at times sacrifice function for perceived status and social dominance (DiDonato & Jakubiak, 2016). Thus, through this perceptual lens, eco-friendly purchasers are viewed as more competent (DiDonato & Jakubiak, 2016). Purchasing green products may also signal values of social responsibility and ethical consciousness to others in the social sphere (Zaharia & Zaharia, 2014). With this in mind, citizens seem to use CSR to advance their own social standing.

Gaining Social Status through CSR Purchases

This social dimension has led consumers to take nonintuitive actions, such as buying inferior products or foregoing luxury items. Consumers seeking better social reputations have purchased green products even though they perceive them as inferior and have done so more readily than buying luxury products (Griskevicius et al., 2010). The impact on the consumer seems to go beyond nontangible status attributes and can lead to attitude changes and actions such as environmental purchasing. Consumers exposed to green products may experience an initial "halo" that allows them to act more altruistically (Mazar & Zhong, 2010). For executives in charge of CSR communication, the language used should focus on the ethical and philanthropic dimensions instead of the positive impact to the bottom line (O'Connor & Shumate, 2010). This approach is advantageous as consumers respond more positively to CSR programs that are "values driven" and not financially driven or part of a green marketing ploy (Ellen et al., 2006). The social dimensions inherent in eco-purchasing involvement provide a platform to understand the potency of consumer-to-consumer communication.

Social media channels offer an environment for the consumer to persuade others to partake in environmental purchasing. Scholars have analyzed the role of social media in the CSR equation. Social media may be especially important to understanding sustainable communications because sustainability is inherently social (Minton et al., 2012). Research has found that pro-social traits are linked with pro-environmental behavior (Kaiser & Byrka, 2011). Consumers who participate in the CSR program's online activities become content creators and can change the perception of the campaign among key stakeholders. Rich media has been shown to have a significant impact on CSR communication (Saat & Selamat, 2014). Scholars have indicated that social media has the effect of creating a collective truth as users generate their own content once the picture is created and shared with others (Aula, 2010). Some argue social media "democratizes" and diversifies CSR communication, thus shaping sustainable communication (Nwagbara & Reid, 2013). The use of social media for a CSR campaign can extend interpersonal communication and lead to the creation of knowledge communities (Kesavan et al., 2013). While gaining gratification from conducting online word of mouth is common among many situations, the preexisting social dimensions of the eco-purchasing involvements resonate with the green consumers. The green consumer is drawn to a green "community" where information sharing is relevant and rewarded. The atmosphere of new media has led to a "dynamization" of communication with a plurality of voices active in social communication (Castello et al., 2013). Scholars have examined the impact of word of mouth in both offline and online environments (Brown & Dacin, 1997; Feng & Papatla, 2011), and have attempted to discern the origin of online communications behavior. Consumers are driven by the desire for social interaction, economic incentives, concern for other consumers, and the potential to enhance their own self-worth when they contemplate electronic word-of-mouth (eWOM) behavior (Hennig-Thurau et al., 2004). Yet scholars have called for further research to determine effective and credible communications channels for CSR programs (Servaes & Tamayo, 2013).

Today consumers and citizens use social media formats to endorse a product attribute, examine ethical behavior, or condemn a corporation for failed products or irresponsible social behavior. The Internet has been called a "great equalizer" in terms of relationship building (Worley, 2007) and has promulgated a new atmosphere for dialogic communication. There is a cacophony of information online leading consumers to struggle to differentiate accurate information from misinformation. In fact, the consumers remain in the center. While traditional CSR campaigns have focused on a traditional sender-receiver model of communication, a new knowledge-sharing orientation is emerging (Chaudri, 2016). Environmentally sensitive consumers are also likely to voice disapproval for a corporation and spread negative word of mouth (Cervellon, 2012). Social media may reduce the incidence of corporate greenwashing as external stakeholders utilize multiple social media forms (Lyon & Montgomery, 2013). As consumers choose information to transmit via social media, they can select from various content formats such as a news release, article, or advertisement, each offering advantages and disadvantages when attempting to convince another consumer to engage in eco-purchasing involvement. Key influencers use all sorts of rich and static media to persuade others.

When considering appropriate formats, it has also been indicated that when conveying CSR, advertising may not be the best approach, and third-party information may be more convincing (Chernev & Blair, 2015). In fact, advertising can have a deleterious effect on the brand if the CSR activity is not consistent with the company's overall corporate reputation (Servaes & Tamayo, 2013). Further, television news can positively influence green purchases (Holbert et al., 2003). The use of assertive commands in environmental communication has also been questioned by researchers (Kronrod et al., 2012), suggesting that less assertive language may be preferable to influence consumers. Scholars have urged researchers to further investigate CSR in an inclusive way by examining stakeholders, focusing on strategic communications models, and evaluating various communications tools to convey messages (Podnar, 2008).

CONTENT CO-CREATION WITH CONSUMER INFLUENCERS: THE SOCIAL MEDIA PARADIGM

While corporations undertake CSR communications for a multitude of reasons, the advent of the consumer communicator empowered with social media requires further analysis. In an effort to promote positive CSR identification with the company, scholars have found that businesses may invite stakeholders to participate and co-construct CSR messages, which leads to greater company-consumer identification (Morsing & Schultz, 2006). By nature of the interaction available through social media, consumers undertake a more active role in communication, conducting word of mouth online and engaging with the company and other consumers in compelling and persuasive ways. Stakeholders are also likely to respond to CSR initiatives based on their own anticipated rewards or benefits (Bhattacharya et al., 2011). Further, social media is considered an ideal medium for green advertisers because consumers can self-select into sustainable lifestyle groups (Minton et al., 2012). It has also been indicated that peer influence provides a powerful predictive factor in green purchase behavior (Lee et al., 2012), indicating electronic word of mouth provides a compelling factor in promoting the reason to buy. Source expertise plays a factor when considering word of mouth (Coulter & Roggeveen, 2012), and the visible source exerts a role in influencing judgments in credibility (Dou et al., 2012), yielding potential impact on the roles of the corporate and consumer communicators. Recommending CSR brands to others may signify good taste by the consumer and illustrate an ethical behavior, thus enhancing status (Wan et al., 2013). The process of recommending purchases by sharing information with others on social media gives the consumer a new activist role, and allows them to harvest the social benefits of the eco-purchasing involvement equation.

By maturing into a more active role, the consumer actively engages with the CSR brand, making judgments and deciding whether or not to embrace an advocacy role. The movements in CSR communication toward co-creation with the stakeholders come at the same time that social media and electronic word of mouth allow for advocacy and thought leadership. The evolution of electronic word of mouth suggests an emerging and more advanced role for the consumer (Hennig-Thurau et al., 2004). A consumer who receives CSR information online will likely make judgments regarding the corporation or the consumer who transmitted the information. In turn, the receiver may make choices on whether to retransmit information or not based on the source credibility. Further, following CSR online exposure, an advocacy role may be exercised as the consumer retransmits information in the form of an article, news release, or advertisement. After viewing CSR information online, the viewer may become an active advocate or opponent to the CSR program. This level of interactivity demonstrates an evaluation of the media format and shows the audience growing as it engages with the company.

Social media environments serve as communication channels for both consumers and corporations. Corporations may use social media outlets to convey corporate messages while consumers come to social media environments to fulfill needs (Gummerus et al., 2012). It may be asserted that environmentalism purchasing behavior may be influenced by the information source or by the media format used to convey the information. The level of engagement may be influenced by the connection between the consumer and corporation, or alternatively the consumer and another consumer. A shared culture may revolve around the product or service that facilitates the communication (Kruckeberg et al., 2006), and this co-creation concept may be applied to CSR information. The type of media format adds a second dynamic to the equation as the receiver may discern aspects of source credibility and information credibility. For example, a consumer may be more likely to retransmit information from a corporation if they feel a strong community connection and that the information is presented in a credible way by using a media format such as an advertisement, article, or news release. It has already been determined that television news has a positive influence on promoting environmentally friendly purchases (Holbert et al., 2003), leading researchers to question the impact of other media formats. By discerning the motivation of the consumer, we may learn about the peer-to-peer environmental purchasing persuasion that occurs via social media. Consumers may satisfy economic and social desires by spreading information through social media (Hennig-Thurau et al., 2004). Therefore, active consumer communicators may enhance their own social status by positioning themselves as experts by sharing specific media content.

Consumers can easily interject their own opinions into comments on social media. Literature points to the new ecosystem of media consumption and media production, fueled by technology and new consumer habits (Jenkins, 2006). Co-creation with audiences is evident leading to new levels of community formation (Korschun & Du, 2013). The willingness of a consumer to engage with a corporation, or another individual, when presented with CSR information may be influenced by a secondary "appeal" by the corporation or by the information. As information spreads virally via social media, personal endorsements, and testimonials may attempt to persuade the individual to engage with the content by liking, sharing, or posting the information. In the social media sphere, engagement can intensify as dialogic communication occurs. Research suggests that this level of engagement may further propel electronic word of mouth (Gummerus et al., 2012). Both the corporation and the consumer play an active role in influencing eco-purchase involvement. Research finds that consumer thought leaders become effective co-creators of content to present a CSR campaign. Scholarship provides managerial insights. Public relations practitioners can interpret several practical lessons. First, corporations engaged in CSR should continue active public relations programs with a solid media relations function to generate news releases and articles that consumers may share via social media. Scholars have also indicated that marketing communications managers in charge of green buying should use "relatable" spokespeople (Gupta & Ogden, 2009), and thus going beyond the corporate spokespeople, selecting consumer spokespeople may offer distinct advantages. Second, corporations should attempt to leverage the social dimensions for the environmental purchasing decision by incentivizing consumers to embrace key CSR messages and share them via social media channels. This underscores existing recommendations for green marketers to emphasize collective gain over self-interest (Gupta & Ogden, 2009). Third, CSR corporations are advised to maintain a strategic communications program that encompasses relationships with media, and allows senior management to formulate relationships with news media. This recommendation is consistent with advice that corporations with active CSR should use communication as a marketing tool by using clear and unambiguous language (Bakar & Ameer, 2011).

ENVIRONMENTAL CONSUMERS AS INFORMATION SOURCES AND CO-CREATORS

In sum, marketers can capitalize on social advantages gained by sharing corporate social responsibility information. Marketing managers may further attempt to leverage that status "gain," convincing consumers to sharing environmentally friendly information and advance CSR brands (Wan et al., 2013). With the consumer communicator acting as a co-creator of marketing content, the professional communicator must find strategic ways to frame messages and promote activity, echoing scholarship that calls for external engagement to promote profitability and to "radically communicate" with the outside world through stakeholder communication (Browne & Nuttal, 2013). While the social media communications channel offers instantaneous peer-to-peer communication, this research further suggests a sustained role for traditional media formats including the news release and article. While corporations may strive for viral social communication of the brand, traditional forms of communication are required to affirm social messages (Kaplan & Haenlein, 2011). The consumer communicator seeking to inform and persuade others about an environmental purchasing decision may transmit an article or a news release instead of an advertisement, allowing them to convey credible brand information and reap the benefits of enhanced social status by participating in the green purchasing decision process.

This chapter indicates how corporations effectively use CSR programs to engage with key publics and encourage them to purchase products. We have explored the role of top-line growth and bottom-line impact for corporate social responsibility programs. Stakeholders play a vital role in communicating specific aspects of CSR programs, promoting trust, and convincing others to make product purchases. Today, consumers reward ethical corporate behavior with payment of higher prices and brand loyalty. Overall, corporations seeking to promote purchase intention through CSR must perform appropriate research and effectively play and implement a strategically sound corporate social responsibility program.

Chapter 7

Measuring Corporate Social Responsibility Programs

Management teams face a daunting challenge when implementing a corporate social responsibility communication effort. How is the corporate social responsibility going to benefit the business? This question opens the door for social media measurement and monitoring, a discreet aspect of public relations measurement that is part of the professional measurement standards for public relations practitioners. It seems then that the traditional adage about what gets measured, gets done, rings true. Despite these best efforts, measurement is a nascent aspect of public relations activities that continues to gain strength and guidance as evidenced by the Barcelona Principles of Measurement, a series of guidelines adopted by global public relations leaders. This chapter explores emerging principles and methodologies for public relations measurement and examines the implementation of social media measurement including sponsorships, celebrity endorsement, and other activities that can lead to a mutually beneficial corporate social responsibility program between the company and various key publics. In particular, you will learn how corporate social responsibility endorsements and their communications activities work to promote CSR platforms, product sales, and branding activities. Further, the chapter explores the heritage and evolution of measurement.

For public relations executives, the ever-present measurement imperative remains. Practitioners advocating for social, economic, or political change remain steadfast in the quest to move the measurement needle, report results, and document the substantive change. In the online sphere, brand ambassadors articulate various brand aspects, demonstrate product attributes and influence many viewers. While at times the marketing heft of key influencers may seem unquantifiable, tools such as the Barcelona Principles of Measurement can provide tangible metrics that allow business executives to make prudent decisions, invest in meaningful online media partnerships, and negotiate winning situations for corporations, end users, and online celebrities. This chapter explores principles of public relations measurement and the current practices of corporate social responsibility communication in a meaningful way for both academia and practical application. The chapter explains the Barcelona Principles of measurement and presents real world examples of brand reputation management online, in particular addressing CEO activism. The Barcelona Principles, originally crafted in 2010, provide an embraced standard for public relations measurement. Public relations professionals have welcomed the guidelines, as appropriate measurement approaches can help professionals gain access to the corporate decision-making table.

The principles were updated in 2015, and again in 2020, to reflect evolving dynamics. The notion of public relations measurement remains a salient topic as executives struggle to measure and monitor the outcomes of specific communication plans. Research has indicated that academics and practitioners can agree to several core concepts to legitimize the measurement and evaluation standards. Specifically, it has been suggested that the standards are necessary to promote comparability and are needed to increase the applicability of research-based measurement and evaluation in organizations, and that aspects of measurement are beneficial to increasing the credibility of the public relations profession (Buhmann et al., 2019). Corporate social responsibility programs must be measured to monitor effectiveness of outcomes. By contemplating the need for measurement prior to launching the program, proper procedures and measurement tools may be put into place.

MEASUREMENT IN PUBLIC RELATIONS

Scholars have indicated that measuring communications enables public relations professionals to meet the demands of senior management, justify allocation of funds, and allow professionals to devise effective communication strategies amid changing circumstances (Argenti, 2006). Practitioners can derive many benefits from measurement, particularly if the results yield insights about the interaction of the organization with its key publics. While scholarship has traditionally focused on public relations measurement executed in connection with a return on investment for brand, product, or issues management, the outcome of engagement as a key metric is required to truly measure the impact of the public relations program (Michaelson & Stacks, 2011). The primary theoretical foundations for social media activities have traditionally focused on engagement, dialogue, transparency, authenticity, and influence (McCorkindale & DiStaso, 2014). While measurement has been elusive at times for public relations activities, practitioners still struggle to find the right measurement approach. Social media now presents a highly quantifiable medium that can trace specific messages to a variety of key publics. However, too often, the measurement activities rely heavily on counting the "who," "what," and "when," using social media monitoring tools and other technology-enabled tools. Yet, to function as a strategic, effective public relations practitioner, the measurement activities must extend beyond simple web analytics to a "deeper dive" to understand the "whys" of behavior (Bartholomew & Chen, 2016). The benefits of measurement are significant, allowing the profession and the individual professional to flourish with the benefit of solid metrics to document the return on communication efforts. Research has indicated that public relations professionals who adopted standardized measurement programs are taken more seriously by the senior management team and can thus gain power over larger strategic decisions and decisions made for the long term (Thorson et al., 2015). When public relations professionals organize and report social media data, they are encouraged to do so in keeping with industry ethical practices and utilize qualitative inquiry methods to articulate the full situation (Place, 2015). Constructing a measurement program is just the beginning, as diligent care is required to implement measurement techniques and report the findings accordingly. A four-pronged model that encompasses measurement, analysis, insights, and evaluation has been proposed as a technique to manage measurement and evaluation (Macnamara, 2014a). This was later elaborated on to create an integrated model of evaluation for strategic communication that looked at an evaluation of an organization's integrated communication by looking through the lens of organizational objectives, communication objectives, inputs, activities, outputs, and outcomes, all while examining the feedback loops in each area (Macnamara, 2018).

Yet despite the overarching sense that public relations professionals need to actively measure program outcomes, professionals and scholars also acknowledge that social media monitoring provides a simple baseline approach that requires more intensive human intervention to provide corresponding analysis and generate the context of the broader impact of communication programs delivered via the channels of social media. The measurement of social media represents an evolution in measurement in public relations, as a move from opinion polls and basic media analysis to more contemporary practices that focus on media outcomes rather than media outputs (Watson, 2012). It has been asserted that traditional media metrics do not translate well to social media, with metrics for "engagement" providing more insightful tools (Bartholomew & Chen, 2016). Macnamara (2014a) suggests an approach to reframe social media metrics to advance from basic output metrics to subsequent "out-takes" and eventual "outcomes." For example, social media "reach" would advance to "likes" and brand impact. Target audience reach may be expressed by followers and awareness. Impressions may be categorized as the out-take of "fans who ultimately form attitudes." A final example is the output metric of share of voice, leading to the out-take of downloads and the outcome of loyalty (Macnamara, 2014b). The measurement mandate sets the stage for a discussion of key influencers who capture the attention of distinct populations, persuading them to try products, gain brand loyalty, or form particular attitudes about issues or services. Amid this backdrop, professionals face new measurement opportunities, particularly in the realm of CSR activities.

The Covid-19 global pandemic prompted corporations to intervene in ways that marketing and communication departments may have never contemplated before. For example, in the early onset of the pandemic private corporations donated personal protective equipment to hospitals and first responders. The need for corporate engagement in respective communities was exposed, recognizing that employees and employers were linked in managing the work world during the global pandemic. Yet steadfast corporate social responsibility programs linked to the environment, global warming, sustainability, combatting food insecurity and hunger, and renewable energy sources remained in place as corporations continue to experience a high level of interactivity with their publics. Corporate management teams found themselves at the center of a global pandemic that required them to make crucial decisions for their employees and the larger community. As we look back at the Carroll Pyramid of corporate social responsibility (Carroll, 1979), the first responsibility to a corporation is to remain profitable, so it in fact can remain in business supplying jobs and economic prosperity to a community. Many corporations found this foundational element harder to accomplish and businesses required creativity to adapt business models and address the pandemic's strain on key stakeholders. With various stakeholders quarantining and turning to online activities for socialization, commerce, and engagement, businesses modified corporate social responsibility programs to the online environment to keep consumers interested and loyal to the brand. With the benefit of social media monitoring tools, corporations could gain a keener eye into the effectiveness of CSR programs and make real-time course corrections in the campaigns that would deliver better overall results.

The Barcelona Principles of Measurement

The Barcelona Principles, as they have been come to be known today, were originally coined the Barcelona Declaration of Research Principles in 2010, a group of tenets agreed upon by public relations practitioners from thirty-three countries who convened at the international Association for Measurement and Evaluation of Communication (AMEC). They have been revised three times and now offer practitioners solid guidelines for program measurement.

The representatives adopted the original declaration of research principles, a set of seven guidelines to measure the effectiveness of public relations campaigns. At the outset, the principles encompassed are (1) recognizing the importance of goal setting and measurement, (2) measuring the effect on outcomes as preferable to measuring outputs, (3) measuring the effect on business results where possible, (4) measuring media incorporating quantity and quality, (5) recognizing advertising value equivalencies AVEs are not the value of public relations, (6) measuring social media, and (7) recognizing transparency and replicability as paramount to sound measurement (AMEC, 2021b). The tenets evolved as practitioners analyzed and practiced them following the 2010 debut.

In a second draft of the Barcelona Principles, the 2.0 version debuted in 2015. The concepts remained in place but evolved to include a wider array of communication types beyond public relations (Rockland, 2015). Through the decadelong introduction and adoption of the principles, practitioners adopted the principles to varying degrees and academics pondered the topics of measurement. The industry observed the evolution of evaluation and discussed the primary role for public relations professionals in evaluation and measurement. Global scholars revisited the Barcelona Principles again in 2020 during a virtual conference, giving way to Barcelona Principles 3.0. The third iteration provides professionals with best practice guidelines for measurement.

Barcelona Principles 3.0

Principle 1: Setting measurable goals is an absolute prerequisite to communication planning, measurement, and evaluation.

Principle 2: Measurement and evaluation should identify outputs, outcomes, and potential impact.

Principle 3: Outcomes and impact should be identified for stakeholders, society, and the organization.

Principle 4: Communication measurement and valuation should include both qualitative and quantitative analysis.

Principle 5: AVEs are not the value of communication.

Principle 6: Holistic communication measurement and evaluation include all relevant online and offline channels.

Principle 7: Communication measurement and evaluation are rooted in integrity and transparency to drive learning and insights.

(Source: Barcelona Principles: https://amecorg.com/2020/07/barcelona-principles-3-0/)

Other Measurement Frameworks

While the Barcelona Principles 3.0 continue to gain acceptance, other measurement frameworks provide tools and resources for public relations practitioners today. The AMEC Integrative Evaluative framework provides an online tool that allows practitioners to enter objectives, outputs, inputs, activities, and out-takes, outcomes, and impact. The objectives are designed to measure the impact of a specific activity such as increases in brand awareness among stakeholders while the outputs are designed to measure various outputs associated with paid, earned, shared, and owned (PESO) media. In the case of a corporate social responsibility program in the social media sphere, observers may count the number of YouTube site views containing the CSR communication. The input section of the evaluative framework allows the users to define the campaign's target audiences and provide general background information about the situation and available resources. For example, a company may seek to advance its corporate social responsibility program by reaching a demographic that overlaps with the company's customer base. The activities portion encompasses research, content, and the specific activities conducted with various media formats. Further, the out-takes portion documents the audience reaction to the activities, attaching various aspects of recall, understanding, and engagement to the discussion. The next two sections identify the outcomes and the impact. By emphasizing the campaign's impact, the effort can be linked to a business outcome or organizational objective. For the company, this may translate into product sales or the audience's participation in a corporate social responsibility program. Public relations professionals have multiple readily available tools to use and today are becoming more skilled at using measurement techniques.

The Institute for Public Relations (IPR) published *The Communicators Guide to Research, Analysis and Evaluation* in March 2021, providing five core competencies in research, analysis, and evaluation: landscape analysis, setting objectives, developing strategy, tactical creation and activation, and evaluation and critical improvement (Institute for Public Relations, 2021). The report, published by the IPR Measurement Commission, acknowledged that technological advances including the advent of artificial intelligence, big data analytics, and behavioral science would propel aspects of engagement between companies and their marketplaces. Amid the changing dynamics, social media measurement has matured. The imperative to analyze the impact of key influencers remains and chief executive officer activism has advanced as chief executive officers become invested in CSR programs.

SOCIAL MEDIA MEASUREMENT

The art of the public relations practice and the science of measurement are now coming together. Public relations scholars have long grappled with the emerging impact of social media on public relations research. Scholars have documented the impact of social media on corporate communication and various aspects of external communication, suggesting a disparity between traditional news media and social media in conveying accurate information in an honest and ethical way (Wright & Hinson, 2009). While much future research may focus on artificial intelligence on social media applications and the power of social media users, academic research between 2006 and 2020 yielded many scholarly journal articles in public relations journals as well as interdisciplinary areas such as new media and media law (Wang et al., 2021). As a burgeoning area, scholars have called for expanded theories to better understand and document the emergence of the social media research in advertising, communication, marketing, and public relations (Khang et al., 2012). The theories used to study social media research often stemmed from theories addressing dialogue, transparency, authenticity, and influence (McCorkindale & DiStaso, 2014). It has been noted that the profession has been gravitating to various standards in an effort to compare campaigns and enhance the overall credibility of the public relations discipline (Buhmann et al., 2019). In the evolving discipline, the emerging power of key influencers presents something that must be measured.

Key Influencer and Measurement of Corporate Social Responsibility Programs

Today, marketers face a daunting challenge to identify and engage with online key influencers. The decision to unite with a particular brand personality can bewilder marketers who seek the enriching, meaningful relationships. Yet how do marketers measure these substantive relationships amid the noise of social media channels and online celebrities? Academic research has shown that the public relations industry has moved to more reliance on audience-specific measurement, thus moving away from output-based measurement to a stance that specifically addresses the audience. Deriving a term from communication studies literature, the term "institutionally effective audiences" reveals that the distinct audience has a social meaning or economic value (Ettema & Whitney, 1994). Yet a simple reliance on volume metrics, as indicated by hits and impressions and other social media metrics, falls short strategically because they only tell a top-line story without interpreting the specific audience effects (Bartholomew & Chen, 2016). Key influencers reach audiences and persuade them to try new products, adopt specific beliefs, and take actions.

As we contemplate the online sphere, the popularity of YouTube celebrities, Facebook thought leaders, and Instagram image makers emerge. The adoption of the Barcelona Principles in 2010 signaled a "reconceptualization" of the public relations industry measurement from outputs to specific outcomes (Chung & Taneja, 2016). Key influencers appear among a broad array of social media channels, offering customer testimonials and endorsements designed to resonate with viewers. Scholarly literature has indicated that social media tactics should be guided by strategic planning, and should revolve around conversations (Plowman & Wilson, 2018). With a focus on conversations, the dialogue with the key influencers will be more "dialogic" and two-way, allowing the viewers to gain a sense of "participation" and community with the thought leader. In fact, social media has given rise to a stronger consumer "public" allowing them to further define the brand by virtue of the interaction with the brand and the key influencer. Let's hypothetically consider an online demonstration of how to utilize a recycled coffee cup, returning the cup for a refill to the coffee retailer. The key influencer demonstrates the benefits of the recycled cup, showing the viewer how to gain maximum benefit from the recycled cup, getting money off the next purchase and preserving the environment. This demonstration then stimulates an online dialogue between the viewer and the key influencer, fostering a sense of community between them and the larger group of viewers, as marketing in the social sphere continues to evolve. The adaptations of marketing in the social environment have led to a rising power of the audience, with corresponding activities that must be measured and monitored by public relations professionals.

Academic research has suggested that three driving forces led to the rising power and prevalence of audience measurement techniques: market conditions, measurement technologies, and the desire for accuracy (Chung & Teneja, 2016). For example, the emergence of web 2.0 environments between 2001 and 2005 created dialogic social platforms whereby corporations could form bonds with customers and thus customer-to-customer communication grew exponentially. To keep pace with the brand marketplace's "social" transformation, online monitoring tools emerged, giving brand marketers more tools in the box to measure engagement and outcomes. Then a subsequent market shift brought social analytics and big data to the fore, further popularizing terms such as "engagement" and "reach." The social media monitoring tools have gained prevalence in brand management, giving marketers "insights" into brand conversations and purchasing behaviors. As social media monitoring advanced in harmony with industry-wide standards for outcome measurement, the desire for accuracy grew, and the reliance on previous metrics of advertising value equivalency (AVEs) gave way to more insightful technologies. In an observation of contemporary marketing trends, we find that corporate social responsibility activities further expand on online sponsorships and celebrity activities. Private monitoring companies are getting into the game by offering analyst-type reports for various industries, as evidenced by Talkwalker's analysis of retail, airline, telecommunications, and food industries with the company's conversational intelligence platform (Talkwalker, 2021). Media company Meltwater acquired Linkfluence, a company that boasts itself as a link between artificial intelligence and market research to deliver key customer insights in various industries such as fashion, food, automotive, entertainment, and sports to help executive management teams monitor reputations, analyze competition, and evaluate campaign performance (Linkfluence, 2021). With the opportunity to decisively measure customer engagement, chief executive officers are formulating CSR programs that will resonate with respective communities and further bind individuals to the company.

MEASUREMENT AND CEO ACTIVISM

Achieving success in today's market requires organizations to transform from a business enterprise to a social enterprise. Hitting the traditional marks of business performance are no longer the only defining metrics of success. Businesses today are being valued as much by their interactions and impacts on society as by their financial results. With that it in mind, we are observing innovative ways that CEO activism is reshaping corporate social responsibility.

Achieving success in today's market requires organizations to transform from a business enterprise to a social enterprise. Hitting the traditional marks of business performance are no longer the only defining metrics of success. Businesses today are being valued as much by their interactions and impacts on society as they are by their financial results. Today, employees and multiple stakeholders are looking to CEOs to lead from the top and have a direct influence in the social policies. So we ask ourselves, "What is the impact of a corporate social responsibility campaign on the corporate reputation? How does this level of engagement take shape in the United States and abroad?" Each year, Edelman Worldwide publishes the Trust Barometer, an annual survey of trust and credibility of four major institutions—the media, governments, corporations, and nongovernment organizations. In what Edelman CEO Richard Edelman called an info-demic, we are currently living in an era whereby citizens to not know where to turn for accurate information. In light of that void, the corporation has stepped up, and in 2021, the employer has become the most trusted source for accurate information (Edelman, 2021).

This finding indicates corporations have an ethical responsibility to effectively communicate with their employees and beyond their walls to the communities in which they operate. Chief executive officers play a vital role in setting the stage for corporate efforts. So let's talk a little bit about CEO activism by looking at Dave Thomas from Wendy's, Richard Branson from Virgin Group, and Sara Blakely from Spanx. Dave Thomas, the founder of Wendy's, leveraged his personal experience with adoption to launch the Dave Thomas Foundation for adoption (Dave Thomas Foundation, 2022). Dave observed a problem with adoption in the U.S. foster care system and sought to unite his corporate wherewithal to address the problem. Every year more than 100,000 children enter the U.S. foster care system and are eligible for foster care adoption because parental rights have been terminated. But only a fraction of those find a permanent home before turning age eighteen. Enter the Dave Thomas Foundation. They started the Wendy's Wonderful Kids Program (WWK) to facilitate permanent foster care adoption. In an overarching effort to raise awareness of this issue, the foundation launched the best adoption-friendly workplace list and has had a substantive impact that has resulted in thousands of children finding permanent homes. President George H. W. Bush named him as a national spokesman on adoption issues, and the Public Relations Society of America awarded a Silver Anvil to the foundation for the national adoption advocacy program. While Dave Thomas passed away in 2002, his daughter Wendy has continued the foundation's work and has a cause marketing effort that allows for proceeds from beverage sales to benefit the foundation and its adoption cause. The integration of this CSR program demonstrates how corporations can leverage a core value and integrate that value system with the corporate behaviors. A second approach we are observing in CEO activism is a strategic focus and attachment to various social issues or causes.

Richard Branson, the founder of Virgin Records and Virgin Atlantic and today the holding company, Virgin Group, is known for his high-profile stunts and also for setting records in powerboat racing and hot-air ballooning. In 2021, he went to music festival South by Southwest to announce the "business leaders against the death penalty declaration" (Galaga, 2021). The declaration was coordinated by the London-based social group Responsible Business Initiative for Justice and was signed by dozens of CEOs, including Ben Cohen and Jerry Greenfield, co-founders of Ben and Jerry's Ice Cream, among others. Amnesty International points to fifty-six countries that still retain the death penalty, and Branson is using his star power to draw attention to this social dilemma. Yet why would Branson make this move? Perhaps we can attribute his actions to a further, advanced approach to corporate social responsibility that "begins at the top," with CEO activism. Another example comes from a female entrepreneur.

In 2006, Sara Blakely launched the Sara Blakely Foundation to help women through education and entrepreneurial training. Richard Branson was one of her first donors, who surprised her with $750,000 check to start the foundation. Since its launch, the Sara Blakely Foundation has funded scholarships for young women. Since its inception, Spanx and the Spanx by Sara Blakely Foundation have been dedicated to elevating and supporting women through entrepreneurship. Knowing the ripple effect that empowering women can have to strengthen communities, the foundation donated $5 million to support female entrepreneurs in the wake of Covid-19 and teamed up with GlobalGiving to establish the Red Backpack Fund. GlobalGiving awarded 1,080 grants of $5,000 each to female entrepreneurs in the United States to help alleviate the impact of the crisis. In 2013, Blakely became the first female billionaire to join the "Giving Pledge," a pledge launched by billionaires Bill Gates and Warren Buffett, whereby the world's most financially wealthy people donate at least half of their wealth to charity (Spanx Foundation, 2022). With chief executive officers taking an active approach to CSR activities, the measurability of CSR programs can come into focus. While CEOs struggle to fund appropriate CSR programs and communicate them effectively, we can look to global leaders for insights. Let's consider the activities of the global company Starbucks.

APPLYING BARCELONA PRINCIPLES 3.0 TO CORPORATE SOCIAL RESPONSIBILITY PROGRAMS

To further explore the Barcelona Principles, let's consider the intersection between the third version of the principles and the corporate social responsibility program underway at Starbucks. If we consider that setting goals is an absolute prerequisite to communication planning, measurement, and evaluation, public relations executives may assign a specific goal and timetable to the objective. Starbucks states the overall corporate goal is to reduce the company's carbon footprint by half by focusing on carbon emissions, waste, and preservation of water (Starbucks, 2022). To illustrate how this may form a communication objective, a realistic goal may be "to increase awareness of the company's environmental efforts among key target market of women age thirty-five to forty-five within one year." The goals themselves may emphasize brand management, catalyzing product sales and promoting engagement with various stakeholders. Principle 2 states that measurement and evaluation should identify outputs, outcomes, and potential impact. For the global Starbucks brand, the output may be articulated as a YouTube video explaining efforts to help farmers cope with environmental change, and the potential impact can be measured by traditional social media metrics *and* resulting consumer behavior including product purchase or participation in in-store activities to promote the initiative. Principle 3 states that outcomes and impact should be identified for stakeholders, society, and the organization. To illustrate this point, it is relevant for the corporation to analyze the increase in sales, stock price, business valuation, and corporate growth catalyzed by the communication. Principle 4 states that communication measurement and valuation should include both qualitative and quantitative analysis. Beyond social media monitoring metrics, it is important to analyze the sentiment and what it "said" on social media, suggesting that a human element is required to prioritize and create context for measurement and evaluation. Principle 5 states that AVEs (advertising value equivalencies) are not the value of communication. For example, it would seem like a stretch to attach an advertising value equivalency to a YouTube video or TikTok that was observed by the brand community. Principle 6 states that holistic communication measurement and evaluation include all relevant online and offline channels. Therefore, the measurement and evaluation of the corporate social responsibility communication must include the totality of the online activities, special events, in-store promotions, celebrity endorsements, and other activities. Lastly, Principle 7 states that communication measurement and evaluation are rooted in integrity and transparency to drive learning and insights. This tenet resonates with corporate communicators responsible for quarterly and annual reporting to a wide range of publics including the management team, investors, vendors, and industry analysts. The compelling value of integrity and transparency further harmonizes with the ethical value codes found in professional public relations societies. In keeping with the Barcelona Principles, the measurement group will recognize that advertising value equivalencies represent a faulty metric and that holistic communication measurement must include online and offline activities, further suggesting a more fulsome approach to measuring integrated marketing communications activities. Lastly, with a focus on integrity and transparency, the company may derive key learnings and benefits that will allow it to retool and thrive in the dynamic, contemporary marketplace.

While public relations professionals continue to grapple with the issues associated with measurement, practitioners lament that the public relations industry still fails to embrace measurement principles and convincingly demonstrate the value of public relations (Macnamara, 2014a). Schriner et al. (2017) indicate that public relations professionals often measure results in terms of "sub outcomes" or interim goals that support the organization's objectives, thus adding another dimension to the measurement dilemma. For evaluation and measurement aspects to thrive in contemporary practice, professionals must embrace the tenets, consider potential intervening variables in campaign effectiveness, and continuously consider the measurement and evaluation models across discrete disciplines such as public relations, investor relations, marketing communications, and next-generation corporate social responsibility. Despite movement in the industry, problems persist including a focus on communication channel activity and the failure to measure events or fully explore behavioral outcomes. At times, practitioners do not embrace appropriate measurement activities and focus instead on communication effects and the channels that were used. By focusing on a tactic, however, practitioners can get off track for more comprehensive, strategic-level decision-making. (Zerfass et al., 2017). It has also been exerted that events and observances require more deliberate measurement, as they may not reveal measurable outcomes as easily (Schriner et al., 2017). Further, research suggests that public relations executives desire insights about social media metrics that analyze more than simple "reach" but extend further to document behavioral outcomes and the true impact on the brand, purchasing behavior, and other aspects including return on investment for communication activities (DiStaso et al., 2011).

Professional communicators (and the entire public relations industry) have a lot to gain through deliberate measurement of communications activities. Notably, the profession can gain more respect and earn a seat at the senior management table, increase funding for activities, and generate better business outcomes (Argenti, 2006). "If you have ever complained that public relations doesn't get a seat at the management table, applying the Barcelona Principles helps the PR and communication functions earn the respect they deserve," said David B. Rockland, in a *Public Relations Tactics* article (Rockland, 2015). However, while public relations practitioners seem willing to participate in holistic measurement activities that utilize both qualitative and quantitative research techniques, they may encounter obstacles when clients are unwilling to invest resources in measurement and evaluation, or they measure the benefits of public relations solely through media relations (Szuba & Tworzydlo, 2020).

The Barcelona Principles propelled a critical shift from measuring outputs to documenting outcomes. Scholars have studied the use of the principles in practice, finding that while they continue to gain acceptance by public relations practitioners in best practice campaigns, ad value equivalencies occasionally persist (Schriner et al., 2017). Measurement has provided an ongoing challenge for public relations professionals as they struggle to uniformly adopt tested theories and models. Further, a lack of engagement and cooperation between public relations industry and academia has endured (Macnamara, 2014b). In sum, the Barcelona Principles 3.0 enlighten discussions about contemporary measurement and evaluation. The use of energy sponsorships and integrations with esports provide a relevant case study in the challenges and opportunities for measurement in the social media era. To effectively implement the Barcelona Principles, corporations and public relations professionals must align objectives and establish intelligent measurement, proper budgets, and consistency (Manning & Rockland, 2011).

While long recognized as a valuable tool in the public relations toolbox, well-embraced methods of uniform measurement have taken decades to take hold. Today, social media and online media convergence creates a new environment that rings a sounding alarm for more robust and meaningful measurement. Methods such as the Barcelona Principles 3.0, the AMEC Integrative Framework, and the IPR's *The Communicator's Guide to Research, Analysis, and Evaluation* provide guideposts for modern-day communication monitoring activities. Further, continued efforts to monitor levels of audience engagement and social media activity will allow a company to measure success when considered in the context of corporate objectives. Armed with solid information, management teams can make appropriate decisions to devise second-generation programs and deliver innovation to the company's corporate social responsibility program.

Chapter 8

The Future of CSR Communication

This book underscores the stakeholder theory of corporate communication. Without enfranchising stakeholders to engage with the corporation, both as a receiver and "relayer" of corporate communication, the corporation misses an opportunity for dynamic communication. The global Covid-19 pandemic brought the urgency for corporate social responsibility campaigns into focus and businesses sought to develop CSR programs that both were strategic and helped the stakeholders relevant to the company. In fact, in what Carroll (2021) called an "energized re-orientation" to CSR, decisions will continue to emanate from the top with varying levels of execution and engagement. Bhattacharya et al. (2009) and Vallaster et al. (2012) have pointed to the imperative for stakeholder involvement.

This book advances those tenets by providing specific insights regarding the role of source, format, and sentiment in creating fertile communications environments for CSR programs. If completed properly, these communication programs can help the company succeed, or conversely, they may fail if communicated ineffectively. The contemporary business atmosphere hums with noise about green advertising messages, the feasibility of corporate social responsibility programs, and the impact of CSR programs on business results. The success or failure of these programs relies on the company's ability to communicate with stakeholders in a meaningful way that fortifies the stakeholder bond. While Carroll (1979) defined corporate social responsibility as a corporation's legal, ethical, environmental, and philanthropic dimensions, communication is ever present in these four factors. For example, to accurately communicate these dimensions in an effort to drive corporate brand reputation and promote purchase intention, companies may transmit public relations content and incentivize consumers to convey information. This book indicates that corporate social responsibility can be a branding tool, as previously reported by Kesavan et al. (2013), and news releases and articles with sentiment are valid ways for a company to convey CSR information to drive the brand. For purchase intention, this book advances communication approaches to build upon the stakeholder-centric model of communication (Bhattacharya et al., 2009) by revealing specific public relations communications techniques that can be used to promote purchase intention.

The text indicates that consumers are playing a more active role in influencing purchasing decisions and that transmitting articles and news releases to consumers, even without a personal sentiment message, can influence the purchasing decision of others. This monitors the evolution into dialogic communication advocated by Kent and Taylor (2002) and demonstrates the involvement of stakeholders in the entire CSR communication process, as advocated by Coombs and Holladay (2012). While businesses may still perform a primary role in conveying corporate information and use corporate spokespeople like the chief executive or a public relations professional, the communication environment allows for the creation of consumer corporate advocates who may use the social media environment for brand advocacy and persuasion of purchasing intention. These findings advance a concept set forth by Marin and Ruiz (2007), who found that CSR propels positive affective, cognitive, and behavioral consumers' responses and that the affective component binds the relationship between the consumer and the corporation.

While corporate social responsibility communication may span multiple disciplines such as marketing, business ethics, and communication studies, this book points to the appropriate engagement of the public relations professional in the corporate social responsibility equation. For public relations professionals to play a powerful role in the communication of corporate social responsibility, they must have access to the decision-making table and leadership for the strategic planning of corporate social responsibility programs. Access to this dominant coalition has been advocated by Broom (2009) and is relevant to the discussion of the role of the public relations professional in corporate social responsibility communication. Coombs and Holladay (2009) have warned that CSR information from another corporate department can be characterized as "encroachment" of a primary business function, and that the role of the public relations professional is paramount. Public relations professionals must have direct access to the chief executive officer and chief operating officer during the formulation of corporate social responsibility initiatives, because public relations executives are keenly aware of the nuances of the various stakeholders. This depth of knowledge and understanding allows public relations professionals to fortify the stakeholder bond through the communication of a prospective corporate social responsibility program. Public relations professionals may combine a multitude of sources, formats, and sentiments to convey information and are likely to utilize the social media sphere to influence stakeholders on corporate social responsibility programs. Today, the public relations industry participates in an environment of engaged, dialogic communication, and practitioners become facilitators of co-creation. While public relations practitioners remain as original content creators of news releases and perform the publicity function for the corporation, as articulated by Grunig and Grunig (1992), they now must perform in a newly evolved role of community builder and facilitator of dialogic co-creation. Public relations professionals may stand on tenets of ethics and community building set forth by Kruckeberg et al. (2006). Through this new role, public relations professionals address and enfranchise the newly empowered consumers to co-create and influence others. The co-creation role, advocated by Korschun and Du (2013), has been shown to reside at the center of stakeholder-centric communication (Bhattacharya et al., 2009). This finding shows that co-creation can be accomplished by creating dialogue networks and institutionalizing dialogic communication in corporate social responsibility programs.

With the solid foundation of ethics in the profession and accreditation, the public relations industry may provide communication leadership in this new era of co-creation. Further, as individuals, they too can articulate person-to-person communication that leverages the news releases and articles created on behalf of the corporation. Thus, while the public relations professional may still serve as an original content creator, to be effective, he or she must deftly reuse and redisseminate traditional media formats of news releases and articles in the social media environment. For determining media credibility, this book affirms concepts of the elaboration likelihood model (Petty & Cacioppo, 1986) that asserts consumers are susceptible to peripheral processing cues. As the postulate on peripheral cues states, these cues take on more importance in processing arguments when motivation is low. The Communication Process Model contained in this book helps public relations practitioners determine effective media sources and formats. While Hallahan (1999) discussed content class as a context clue for information processing when comparing publicity versus advertising, this book advances the discussion by evaluating the social media environment within the context of a corporate social responsibility program. In addition, the effect of sentiment is also evaluated in communication processing. Morsing and Schultz (2006) called for involving CSR stakeholders in the communication process. This book provides specific techniques for a corporation to convey information and reveals source/sentiment formats that are likely to be used in the social media environment. While consumers in the social media environment may be driven by the desire for social interaction, economic incentives, concern for other customers, and concern for self-worth (Hennig-Thureau et al., 2004), this book sheds new light on the formats that they may be willing to transmit via social media. By enfranchising the stakeholder, the corporation can further maximize communication of the CSR program. In sum, the implications for corporate social responsibility communication, the public relations profession, and institutional social media engagement require a new model for CSR communication.

"Communication precedes commerce." This book comes at a time when corporations are facing pressures to devise and implement corporate social responsibility programs and deal with a global pandemic. From multinational corporations to small independent retailers, businesses are facing increasing CSR pressures as consumers become more demanding for social programs that allow for greater interactivity between the corporation and the community. The ubiquity of social media has added a new ingredient for corporate communicators who want to broadcast the elements of a corporate social responsibility program. While Carroll (1979) has called CSR a company's economic, legal, ethical, and philanthropic responsibility, CSR communication is now conducted in a landscape of social media where co-creation with the audience occurs twenty-four hours a day, seven days a week. How companies choose to communicate with their key stakeholders may mean the difference between success or failure of a specific program. If the appropriate source, format, and sentiment are used, then the corporation may be able to enhance its corporate brand reputation or impact the bottom line by promoting purchasing intention. Yet the issues of source credibility and information credibility remain.

Public relations professionals, the primary message framers who maintain intimate knowledge of a corporation's primary and secondary stakeholders, remain aptly poised to lead corporate CSR communication. This book underscores the imperative for an active public relations campaign that generates news releases, and supports the notion of a media relations campaign. Yet public relations professionals must go beyond the traditional press agentry role to a strategic framer of the corporation's corporate social responsibility messages. This expanded role for the public relations professional has been endorsed by scholars (Daugherty, 2001; Freitag, 2005), and this book advances these argument for the public relations professional's active involvement in conveying contents in the social media environment. This book paves the way for a deeper understanding of the role of the public relations professional in formulating, executing, and measuring a strategic communication program for corporate social responsibility. This book indicates that as the industry continues its evolution in the dialogic era, the public relations professional has the opportunity to become a maestro of communication, characterized as one who can inspire other consumer users to carry the message in a powerful electronic word-of-mouth channel. Public relations executives must frame the message, conduct media relations, counsel the chief executives, and communicate as an individual using appropriate social media vehicles. Yet the public relations professional, with a keen sense of the stakeholder base, and bound by a strong sense of professional ethics, can navigate the formation and execution of a corporate social responsibility communication program. This book offers implications for corporate social responsibility communication and theory, as a new era of dialogic communication pervades the marketplace and dictates that corporations utilize the social media channels to convey information and engage with stakeholders. For the public relations industry, this text articulates a valid argument for the public relations professional at the highest level of strategic planning and leader of implementation. The public relations professional may serve as a primary creator of corporate CSR communication, with research finding that the corporation can derive significant benefits of corporate brand reputation, purchase intention, source credibility, information credibility, and social media engagement by transmitting news releases and articles through social media outlets. A five-phase Corporate Social Responsibility Communication Model is proposed that presents a contemporary framework for businesses to apply best practices for CSR communication. The model considers the contemporary communication environment that is characterized by a blending of content creation, giving noncorporate speakers new channels for instantaneous communication. This is particularly relevant for the study of corporate social responsibility, as consumer citizens become watchdogs, brand advocates, and critics of CSR programs. We live in an interconnected world where business, politics, and economics overlap for the welfare of nations and the world. Communication resides at the center of these paradigms and elements of persuasion must be considered as the source, the media format, and the use of sentiment are employed. This work contributes to the body of knowledge of corporate social responsibility communication and offers a direct call for public relations professionals to take the helm with senior executives.

Bibliography

AbbVie (2022). AbbVie's response to COVID-19. https://www.abbvie.com/coronavirus.html

Ahmad, N., Naveed, R. T., Scholz, M., Irfan, M., Usman, M., & Ahmad, I. (2021). CSR communication through social media: A litmus test for banking consumers' loyalty. *Sustainability*, 13(4), 2319.

Airbnb (2022). In times of crisis be a host. https://www.airbnb.org/refugees

Allagui, I., & Breslow, H. (2016). Social media for public relations: Lessons from four effective cases. *Public Relations Review*, 42(1), 20–30.

AMEC (2021a). Integrated Evaluation Framework. Retrieved https://amecorg.com/amecframework/

AMEC (2021b). Barcelona Principles 3.0. Retrieved https://amecorg.com/resources/barcelona-principles-3-0/

AMEC (2022). International Association for the Measurement and Evaluation of Communication. Barcelona Principles 3.0. https://amecorg.com/2020/07/barcelona-principles-3-0

Araujo, T., & Kollat, J. (2018). Communicating effectively about CSR on Twitter: The power of engaging strategies and storytelling elements. *Internet Research*, 28(2), 419–431.

Argenti, P. (2005, Spring). The strategic communication imperative. *MIT Sloan Management Review*, 83–89.

Argenti, P. (2006). Communications and business value: Measuring the link. *Journal of Business Strategy*, 27(6), 29–40.

Argenti, P. A. (2009). Digital strategies for powerful corporate communications. New York: McGraw-Hill.

Auger, P., Burke, P., Devinney, T., & Louviere, J. (2003). What will consumers pay for social product features? *Journal of Business Ethics*, 42(3), 281–304.

Aula, P. (2010). Social media, reputational risk and ambient publicity management. *Strategy and Leadership*, 38(6), 43–49.

Bakar, A., & Ameer, R. (2011). Readability of corporate social responsibility communication in Malaysia. *Corporate Social Responsibility and Environmental Management*, 18, 50–60.

Bamberg, S. (2003). How does environmental concern influence specific environmentally related behaviors? A new answer to an age-old question. *Journal of Environmental Psychology*, 23(1), 21–32.

Bartholomew, D., & Chen, Z. F. (2016). Thus spoke the measurati. In Z. Chen, ed. *MetricsMan: It Doesn't Count Unless You Can Count It*, 151–174. Business Expert Press.

Basu, K., & Palazzo, G. (2008). Corporate social responsibility: A process model of sensemaking. *Academy of Management Review*, 33(1), 122–136.

Batanic, B., & Appel, M. (2013). Mass communication, social influence, and consumer behavior: Two field experiments. *Journal of Applied Social Psychology*, 43, 135–168.

Becker-Olsen, K., Cudmore, A., & Hill, R. (2006). The impact of perceived corporate social responsibility on corporate behavior. *Journal of Business Research*, 59(1), 46–53.

Benn, S., & Bolton, D. (2011). *Key concepts in corporate social responsibility*. Thousand Oaks: Sage.

Benn, S., Todd, L., & Pendleton, J. (2010). Public relations leadership in corporate social responsibility. *Journal of Business Ethics*, 96, 403–423.

Bhattacharya, C., & Korschun, D. (2008). Beyond the four P's and the consumer. *Journal of Public Policy and Marketing*, 27(1), 113–116.

Bhattacharya, C., Korschun, D., & Sen, S. (2009). Strengthening stakeholder company relationships through mutually beneficial corporate social responsibility initiatives. *Journal of Business Ethics*, 85(Supplement 2), 257–272.

Bhattacharya, C., & Sen, S. (2003). Consumer-company identification: A framework for understanding consumers' relationships with companies. *The Journal of Marketing*, 67(2), 76–88.

Bhattacharya, C., Sen, S., & Korschun, D. (2011). *Leveraging corporate social responsibility: The stakeholder route to maximizing business and social value*. New York: Cambridge University Press.

Bivins, T. (1993). Public relations, professionalism, and the public interest. *Journal of Business Ethics*, 12(2), 117–126.

Boadi, E., He, Z., Bosompem, J., Say, J., & Boadi, E. K. (2019). Let the talk count: Attributes of stakeholder engagement, trust, perceive environmental protection and CSR. *Sage Open*, 9(1), 2158244019825920.

Brengman, M., & Karimov, F. (2012). The effect of web communities on consumers' initial trust in B2C ecommerce websites. *Management Research Review*, 35(9), 791–816.

Broom, G. M. (2009). *Cutlip and Center's effective public relations*. Upper Saddle River: Pearson Education.

Brown, J., Broderick, A., & Lee, N. (2007). Word of mouth communication within online communities: Conceptualizing the online social metwork. *Journal of Interactive Marketing*, 21(3), 2–20.

Brown, T., & Dacin, P. (1997). The company and the product: Corporate associations and consumer product responses. *Journal of Marketing*, 61(1), 68–84.

Browne, J., & Nuttal, R. (2013). Beyond corporate social responsibility: Integrating external engagement. *McKinsey Quarterly*, April 1–11.

Browning, N., Lee, E., Park, Y. E., Kim, T., & Collins, R. (2020). Muting or meddling? Advocacy as a relational communication strategy affecting organization-public relationships and stakeholder response. *Journalism & Mass Communication Quarterly*, 97(4), 1026–1053.

Bruhn, M., Schoenmueller, V., & Schafer, D. (2012). Are social media replacing traditional media in terms of brand equity creation? *Management Research Review*, 35(9), 770–790.

Buhmann, A., Likely, F., & Geddes, D. (2018). Communication evaluation and measurement: Connecting research to practice. *Journal of Communication Management*, 22(1), 113–119.

Buhmann, A., Macnamara, J., & Zerfass, A. (2019). Reviewing the "march to standards" in public relations: A comparative analysis of four seminal measurement and evaluation initiatives. *Public Relations Review*, 45(4), DOI 10.1016/j.pubrev.2019.101825.

Byrum, K. (2017). Boosting brand reputation and promoting purchase intention through corporate social responsibility communication: A test of source, format and sentiment effects in social media. *Research Journal of the Institute for Public Relations*, 3(2), 1–20.

Campbell's (2022). Campbell's corporate social responsibility strategy. https://www.campbellcsr.com/cr-at-campbell/strategy.html

Capriotti, P., & Moreno, A. (2007). Corporate citizenship and public relations: The importance and interactivity of social responsibility issues on corporate websites. *Public Relations Review*, 33(1), 84–91.

Carroll, A. (1979). A three-dimensional conceptual model of corporate social performance. *Academy of Management Review*, 4(4), 497–505.

Carroll, A. B. (2021). Corporate social responsibility (CSR) and the COVID-19 pandemic: Organizational and managerial implications. *Journal of Strategy and Management*, 14(3), 315–330.

Castello, I., Morsing, M., & Schultz, F. (2013). Communicative dynamics and the polyphony of corporate social responsibility in the network society. *Journal of Business Ethics*, 118, 683–694.

CBRE (2022). Corporate social responsibility report 2020. https://www.cbre.com/-/media/files/corporate%20responsibility/cr%20report/2020/cbre_2020_cr_report.pdf

Cervellon, M. (2012). Victoria's dirty secrets: Effectiveness of green not-for-profit messages targeting brands. *Journal of Advertising*, 41(4), 133–145.

Chaudri, V. (2016). Corporate social responsibility and the communication imperative: Perspectives from CSR managers. *International Journal of Business Communication*, 53(4), 1–24.

Chen, Y. S. (2008). The driver of green innovation and green image—green core competence. *Journal of Business Ethics*, 81(3), 531–543.

Chen, Y. S. (2010). The drivers of green brand equity: Green brand image, green satisfaction, and green trust. *Journal of Business Ethics*, 93(2), 307–319.

Cheng, Y., Wang, Y., Zhao, W., Zhang, K., Cai, X., & Jiang, H. (2022). Virtually Enhancing Public Engagement During the Pandemic: Measuring the Impact of Virtual Reality Powered Immersive Videos on Corporate Social Responsibility Communication. *Social Science Computer Review*, 0(0). https://doi.org/10.1177/08944393221111482

Chernev, A., & Blair, S. (2015). Doing well by doing good: The benevolent halo of corporate social responsibility. *Journal of Consumer Research*, 41(6), 1412–1425.

Cho, S., & Hong, Y. (2008). Netizens' evaluation of corporate social responsibility: Content analysis of CSR news stories and online readers' comments. *Public Relations Review*, 35(2), 147–149.

Chu, S., & Chen, H. (2019). Impact of consumers' corporate social responsibility-related activities in social media on brand attitude, electronic word-of-mouth intention, and purchase intention: A study of Chinese consumer behavior. *Journal of Consumer Behaviour*, 18(6), 453–462.

Chung, S., & Taneja, H. (2016). Reassessment of audience in the public relations industry: How social media reshape public relations measurements. *Asia Pacific Public Relations Journal*, 17(1), 60–77.

Clark, C. (2000). Differences between public relations and corporate social responsibility: An analysis. *Public Relations Review*, 26(3), 263–280.

Coombs, T., & Holladay, S. (2012). *Managing corporate social responsibility: A communication approach*. Malden: Wiley-Blackwell.

Coombs, W., & Holladay, S. (2009). Corporate social responsibility: Missed spportunity for institutionalizing communication practice? *International Journal of Strategic Communication*, 3(2), 93–101.

Coulter, K., & Roggeveen, K. (2012). "Like it or not": Consumer responses to word-of-mouth communication in on-line social networks. *Management Research Review*, 35(9), 878–899.

Creyer, E., & Ross, W. (1996). The influence of firm behavior on purchase intention: Do consumers really care about business ethics? *Journal of Consumer Marketing*, 14(6), 421–431.

Cutler, A. (2004). Methodological failure: The use of case study method by public relations researchers. *Public Relations Review*, 30(3), 365–375.

Daugherty, E. (2001). Public relations and social responsibility. In R. Heath, ed., *Handbook of Public Relations* (pp. 389–402). Thousand Oaks: Sage.

Dave Thomas Foundation. (2022). Finding forever families for children in foster care. https://www.davethomasfoundation.org/

David, P., Kline, S., & Dai, Y. (2005). Corporate social responsibility practices, corporate identity and purchase intention: A dual process model. *Journal of Public Relations Research*, 17(3), 291–313.

Dean, D. (2002). Associating the corporation with a charitable event through sponsorship: Measuring the effects on corporate community relations. *Journal of Advertising*, 31(4), 77–87.

DiDonato, T., & Jakubiak, B. (2016). Sustainable decisions signal sustainable relationships: How purchasing decisions affect perceptions and romantic attraction. *The Journal of Social Psychology*, 156(1), 8–27.

Diermeier, D. (2011). *Reputation rules: Strategies for building your company's most valuable asset*. New York: McGraw-Hill.

DiStaso, M. W., McCorkindale, T., & Wright, D. K. (2011). How public relations executives perceive and measure the impact of social media in their organizations. *Public Relations Review*, 37(3), 325–328.

Doran, C. (2009). The role of personal values in fair trade consumption. *Journal of Business Ethics*, 84(4), 549–563.

Dou, X., Walden, J., Lee, S., & Lee, J. (2012). Does source matter? Examining source effects in online product reviews. *Computers in Human Behavior*, 28(5), 1555–1563.

Dove (2022). Take care, be safe: How we're caring for our community. https://www.dove.com/us/en/stories/about-dove/take-care-be-safe.html

Dowling, G., & Moran, P. (2012). Corporate reputations. *California Management Review*, 54(2), 25–42.

Dozier, D. G. (1995). *Manager's guide to excellence in public relations and communication management*. Mahwah: Lawrence Erlbaum Associates.

Du, S., Battacharya, C., & Sen, S. (2010). Maximizing business returns to corporate social responsiblity (CSR): The role of CSR communications. *International Journal of Management Review*, 12(1), 8–19.

Dunn, K., & Harness, D. (2018). Communicating corporate social responsibility in a social world: The effects of company-generated and user-generated social media content on CSR attributions and skepticism. *Journal of Marketing Management*, 34(17–18), 1503–1529.

Edelman (2021). 2021 Edelman Trust Barometer. Retrieved https://www.edelman.com/trust/2021-trust-barometer

Elkington, J. (1997). *Cannibals with forks*. Oxford: Capstone.

Ellen, P., Webb, D., & Mohr, L. (2006). Building corporate associations: Consumer attributions for corporate socially responsible programs. *Journal of the Academy of Marketing Science*, 34(2), 147–157.

Ettema, J. S., & Whitney, D. (Eds). (1994). *Audiencemaking: How the media create the audience*. Thousand Oaks: Sage.

Falck, O., &. Heblich, S. (2007). Corporate social responsibility: Doing well by doing good. *Business Horizons*, 50(3), 247–254.

Feng, J., & Papatla, P. (2011). Advertising: Stimulant or suppressant of online word of mouth. *Journal of Interactive Marketing*, 25(2), 75–84.

Fitzpatrick, K., & Gauthier, C. (2011). Toward a professional responsibility theory of public relations ethics. *Journal of Mass Media Ethics: Exploring Questions of Media Morality*, 16(2–3), 193–212.

Flanagin, A., & Metzger, M. (2000). Perceptions of internet information credibility. *Journalism and Mass Communications Quarterly*, 77(3), 515–540.

Folkes, V. (1988). Recent attribution research in consumer behavior: A review and new directions. *Journal of Consumer Research*, 14(4), 548–565.

Fombrun, C., & Shanley, M. (1990). What's in a name: Reputation building and corporate Strategy. *The Academy of Management Journal*, 33(2), 233–258.

Freitag, A. (2005). Staking claim: Public relations leaders needed to shape CSR policy. *Public Relations Quarterly*, 52(1), 37–40.

Galaga, O. (2021). Richard Branson announces anti-death penalty initiative in SXSW panel. https://www.austin360.com/story/entertainment/music/sxsw/2021/03/18/sxsw-richard-branson-death-penalty-capital-punishment-initiative/4753853001/

Gaziano, C., & McGrath, K. (1986). Measuring the Concept of Credibility. *Journalism Quarterly*, 63(3), 451–462.

General Mills (2022). Covid-19 and our communities. https://globalresponsibility.generalmills.com/HTML1/general_mills-global_responsibility_2021_0063.htm

Gensler, S., Volckner, F., Yuping, L., & Wiertz, C. (2013). Managing brands in the social media environment. *Journal of Interactive Marketing*, 27(14), 242–256.

Giacalone, R., Paul, K., & Jurkiewicz, C. (2005). A preliminary investigation into the role of positive psychology in consumer sensitivity to corporate social performance. *Journal of Business Ethics*, 58(4), 295–305.

Golan, G. J. (2010). New perspectives on media credibility research. *American Behavioral Scientist*, 54(1), 3–7.

Good, J. (2006). Internet use and environmental attitude. A social capital approach. In S. P. Depoe, ed., *The Environmental Communication Yearbook, vol. 3,* (pp. 211–233). New York: Routledge.

Green, T., & Peloza, J. (2011). How does corporate social responsibility create value for consumers? *Journal of Consumer Marketing*, 28(1), 48–56.

Greer, J. D. (2003). Evaluating the credibility of online information: A test of source and advertising influence. *Mass Communication and Society*, 6(1), 11–28.

Griskevicius, V., Tybur, J. M., & Van den Bergh, B. (2010). Going green to be seen: status, reputation, and conspicuous conservation. *Journal of Personality and Social Psychology*, 98(3), 392.

Grunig, J., & Grunig, L. (1992). Models of public relations and communications. In J. Grunig, ed., *Excellence in Public Relations Management and Communications Management* (pp. 285–324). Hillsdale: Lawrence Erlbaum Associates.

Gummerus, J., Likljander, V., Weman, E., & Pihlstrom, M. (2012). Customer engagement in a Facebook brand community. *Management Research Review*, 35(9), 857–877.

Gupta, S., Nawaz, N., Alfalah, A. A., Naveed, R. T., Muneer, S., & Ahmad, N. (2021). The relationship of CSR communication on social media with consumer purchase intention and brand admiration. *Journal of Theoretical & Applied Electronic Commerce Research*, 16(5), 1217–1230.

Gupta, S., Nawaz, N., Tripathi, A., Muneer, S., & Ahmad, N. (2021). Using social media as a medium for CSR communication, to induce consumer-brand relationship in the banking sector of a developing economy. *Sustainability*, 13(7), 3700.

Gupta, S., & Ogden, D. (2009) To buy or not to buy, a social dilemma perspective on green buying. *Journal of Consumer Marketing*, 26(6), 376–391.

Hall, M. (2006). Corporate philanthropy and corporate community relations. *Journal of Public Relations Research*, 18(1), 1–21.

Hall, S. (1980). Encoding/decoding. In S. Hall, D. Hobson, A. Lowe, & P. Willis, eds., *Culture, Media, Language: Working Papers in Cultural* Studies, 1972–1979, Ch. 10. Birmingham: Hutchinson Group.
Hallahan, K. (1999). Content class as a contextual cue in the cognitive processing of publicity versus advertising. *Journal of Public Relations Research*, 11(4), 293–320.
Hamlin, R., & Wilson, T. (2004). The impact of cause branding on consumer reactions to products: Does product/cause "fit" really matter? *Journal of Marketing Management*, 20(7–8), 663–681.
Hennig-Thurau, T., Gwinner, K., Walsh, G., & Gremler, D. (2004). Electronic word-of-mouth via consumer-opinion platforms: What motivates consumers to articulate themselves on the Internet? *Journal of Interactive Marketing*, 18(1), 39–52.
Hesari, A. E., & Shadiardehaei, E. (2021). The effect of corporate social responsibility on brand performance with the mediating role of corporate reputation, resource commitment and green greativity. *Tehnički glasnik*, 15(1), 84–91.
Holbert, R. L., Kwak, N., & Shah, D. (2003). Environmental concerns, patterns of television viewing and pro environmental factors: Integrating models of media consumption and effects. *Journal of Broadcasting and Electronic Media*, 47(2), 177–196.
Hovland, C., & Weiss, W. (1951). The influence of source credibility on communication effectiveness. *The Public Opinion Quarterly*, 15(4), 635–650.
Hsuan-Hsuan, K., Chien-Chih, K., Ching-Luen, W., & Chih-Ying, W. (2012). Communicating green marketing appeals effectively. *Journal of Advertising*, 41(4), 41–50.
Huang, Y. (2004). Is symmetrical communication ethical and effective? *Journal of Business Ethics*, 53(4), 333–352.
Institute for Public Relations (2021). *The communicator's guide to research, analysis, and evaluation*. Retrieved https://instituteforpr.org/communicators-guide-research-2021/
Intel (2022). Leveraging technology to provide global pandemic relief. https://www.intel.com/content/www/us/en/newsroom/opinion/leveraging-technology-global-pandemic-relief.html
Jahdi, K., & Acikdilli, G. (2009). Marketing communications and corporate social responsibility (CSR): Marriage of convenience or shotgun wedding? *Journal of Business Ethics*, 88(1), 103–113.
Jenkins, H. (2006). *Convergence culture where old and new media collide*. New York: New York University Press.
Jiang, Y., & Park, H. (2022, March 1). Mapping networks in corporate social responsibility communication on social media: A new approach to exploring the influence of communication tactics on public responses. *Public Relations Review*, 48(1), 102–143.
Johansen, T., & Nielsen, A. (2011). Strategic stakeholder dialogues: A discursive perspective on relationship building. *Corporate Communications: An International Journal*, 16(3), 204–217.

Kaiser, F. G., & Byrka, K. (2011). Environmentalism as a trait: Gauging people's pro-social personality in terms of environmental engagement. *International Journal of Psychology*, 46(1), 71–79.

Kaplan, A., & Haenlein, M. (2011). Two hearts in three-quarter time: How to waltz the social media/viral marketing dance. *Business Horizons*, 54(3), 253–263.

Katz, E., & Lazarsfeld, P. (1955). *Personal influence.* New York: The Free Press.

Kennedy, G. (Trans.). (2007). *Aristotle on rhetoric: A theory of civic discourse.* New York: Oxford University Press.

Kent, M., & Taylor, M. (1998). Building dialogic relationships through the World Wide Web. *Public Relations Review*, 24(3), 321.

Kent, M., & Taylor, M. (2002). Toward a dialogic theory of public relations. *Public Relations Review*, 28(3), 21–37.

Kesavan, R., Bernacchi, M., & Mascarenhas, O. (2013). Word of mouse: CSR communication and social media. *International Management Review*, 9(1), 58–63.

Khang, H., Ki, E., & Ye, L. (2012). Social media research in advertising, communication, marketing, and public relations, 1997–2010. *Journalism and Mass Communications Quarterly*, 89(2), 279–298.

Kim, D., Song, Y., Braynov, S., & Rao, H. (2005). A multidimensional trust formation model in B-to-C e-commerce: A conceptual framework and content analyses of academia/practitioner perspectives. *Decision Support Systems*, 40(2), 143–165.

Kim, H., & Xu, H. (2019). Exploring the effects of social media features on the publics' responses to decreased usage CSR messages. *Corporate Communications: An International Journal*, 4(2), 287–302.

Kim, S. (2011). Transferring effects of CSR strategy on consumer responses: The synergistic model of corporate communication strategy. *Journal of Public Relations Research*, 23(2), 218–241.

Kim, S., & Reber, B. (2008). Public relations' place in corporate social responsibility: Practitioners define their role. *Public Relations Review*, 34(3), 337–342.

Kiousis, S., Popescu, C., & Mitrook, M. (2011). Understanding influence on corporate reputation: An examination of public relations efforts, media coverage, public opinion, and financial performance from an agenda-building and agenda-setting perspective. *Journal of Public Relations Research*, 19(2), 147–165.

Kollmuss, A., & Agyeman, J. (2002). Mind the Gap: Why do people act environmentally and what are the barriers to pro-social behavior? *Environmental Education Research*, 8(3), 239–260.

Korschun, D., & Du, S. (2013). How virtual corporate social responsibility dialogs generate value: A framework and propositions. *Journal of Business Research*, 66(9), 1494–1504.

Kraak, V. I., Davy, B. M., Rockwell, M. S., Kostelnik, S., & Hedrick, V. E. (2020). Policy recommendations to address energy drink marketing and consumption by vulnerable populations in the United States. *Journal of the Academy of Nutrition and Dietetics*, 120(5), 767–777.

Kronrod, A., Grinstein, A., & Wathieu, L. (2012). Go green! Should environmental messages be so assertive? *Journal of Marketing*, 76 (January), 95–102.

Kruckeberg, D. (1996). Transnational corporate ethical responsibilities. In H. M Culbertson & N. Chen, eds., *International Public Relations: A Comparative Analysis* (pp. 81–92). Mahwah: Lawrence Erlbaum Associates.

Kruckeberg, D., Starck, K., & Vujnovic, M. (2006). The role and ethics of community-building for consumer products and services. In C. H. Botan, ed., *Public Relations Theory II* (pp. 485–498). Mahwah: Lawrence Erlbaum Associates.

Ku, H., Kuo, C., Wu, C., & Wu, C. (2012). Communicating green marketing appeals effectively. *Journal of Advertising*, 41(4), 41–50.

Kwok, M., Wong, M., & Lau, M. (2015). Examining how environmental concern affects purchase intention: Mediating role of perceived trust and moderating role of perceived risk. *Contemporary Management Research*, 11(2), 143–152.

Lee, E., & Yoon, S. (2018). The effect of customer citizenship in corporate social responsibility (CSR) activities on purchase intention: The important role of the CSR image. *Social Responsibility Journal*, 14(4), 753–763.

Lee, E. M., Park, S. Y., Rapert, M. I., & Newman, C. L. (2012). Does perceived consumer fit matter in corporate social responsibility issues? *Journal of Business Research*, 65(11), 1558–1564.

Lee, S. Y., Zhang, W., & Abitbol, A. (2019). What makes CSR communication lead to CSR participation? Testing the mediating effects of CSR associations, CSR credibility, and organization-public relationships. *Journal of Business Ethics*, 157(2), 413–429.

Leeper, R. (2001). In search of a metatheory for public relations. In *Handbook of Public Relations* (pp. 93–104). Thousand Oaks: Sage.

Leonidou, C., Katskeas, C., & Morgan, N. (2013). "Greening" the marketing mix: Do firms do it and does it pay off? *Journal of the Academy of Marketing Science*, 41(2), 151–170.

L'Etang, J. (1994). Public relations and corproate social responsibility: Some issues arising. *Journal of Business Ethics*, 13(2), 111–123.

Li, C. (2013). Persuasive messages on information system acceptance: A theoretical extension of elaboration likelihood model and social influence theory. *Computers in Human Behavior*, 29(1), 264–275.

Linkfluence (2021). We're joining forces with Meltwater to accelerate our leadership in AI-enabled consumer insights. https://www.linkfluence.com/blog/linkfluence-is-joining-forces-with-meltwater

Liu, X., Mao, L., & Deng, W. (2018). The influence of consumer mindset and corporate social responsibility on purchase intention. *Social Behavior and Personality*, 46(10), 1647–1655.

Lopez, M., & Sicilia, M. (2013). How WOM marketing contributes to new product adoption. *European Journal of Marketing*, 47(7), 1089–1114.

Luo, X., & Bhattacharya, C. B. (2006). Corporate social responsibility, customer satisfaction, and market value. *Journal of Marketing*, 70(4), 1–18.

Lyft (2022). Lyft's 2021 environmental, social, and corporate governance report. https://www.lyft.com/blog/posts/lyfts-2021-esg-report

Lyon, T., & Montgomery, A. (2013). Tweetjacked: The impact of social media on corporate greenwash. *Journal of Business Ethics*, 118, 747–757.

Macnamara, J. (2014a). Breaking the measurement and evaluation deadlock: A new approach and model. *Journal of Communication Management*, 19(4), 371–387.

Macnamara, J. (2014b). Emerging international standards for measurement and evaluation of public relations: A critical analysis. *Public Relations Inquiry*, 3(1), 7–29.

Macnamara, J. (2018). A review of new evaluation models for strategic communication: Progress and gaps. *International Journal of Strategic Communication*, 12(2), 180.

Mahmud, A., Ding, D., & Hasan, M. M. (2021). Corporate social responsibility: Business responses to coronavirus (COVID-19) pandemic. *SAGE Open*, 11(1), 2158244020988710.

Maignan, I., & Ferrell, O. (2004). Corporate social responsibility and marketing: An integrative framework. *Journal of the Academy of Marketing Science*, 32(1), 3–19.

Manning, A., & Rockland, D. B. (2011). Understanding the Barcelona Principles. *Public Relations Strategist*, 17(1), 30–31.

Marin, L., & Ruiz, S. (2007). "I need you too!": Corporate identity attractiveness for consumers and the role of social responsibility. *Journal of Business Ethics*, 71(3), 245–260.

Marin, L., Ruiz, S., & Rubio, A. (2009). The role of identity salience in the effects of corporate social responsibility on consumer behavior. *Journal of Business Ethics*, 84(1), 65–78.

Mazar, N., & Zhong, C. B. (2010). Do green products make us better people? *Psychological Science*, 21(4), 494–498.

McCorkindale, T., & DiStaso, M. (2014). The state of social media research: Where we are now, where we were and what it means for public relations. *Research Journal of the Institute for Public Relations*, 1(1), 1–17.

Metzger, M. (2007). Making sense of credibility on the web: Models for evaluating online information and recommendations for future research. *Journal of the American Society for Information Science and Technology*, 58(13), 2078–2091.

Michaelson, D., & Stacks, D. (2011). Standardization in public relations measurement and evaluation. *Public Relations Journal*, 5(2), 1–22.

Microsoft (2022). An updated on our AI for health program. https://blogs.microsoft.com/on-the-issues/2020/11/09/ai-for-health-covid-19-update/

Minton, E., Lee, C., Orth, U., Kim, C., & Kahle, L. (2012). Sustainable marketing and social media: A cross country analysis of motives for sustainable behaviors. *Journal of Advertising*, 41(4), 69–84.

Mohr, L., &.Webb, D. (2005). The effects of corporate social responsibility and price on consumer responses. *The Journal of Consumer Affairs*, 39(1), 121–147.

Morsing, M., & Schultz, M. (2006). Corporate social responsibility communication: Stakeholder information, response and involvement strategies. *Business Ethics: A European Review*, 15(4), 323–338.

Moser, A. (2015). Thinking green, buying green? Drivers of pro-environmental purchasing behavior. *Journal of Consumer Marketing*, 32(3), 167–175.

Murray, K., & Vogel, C. (1997). Using a hierarchy-of-effects approach to gauge the effectiveness of corporate social responsbility to generate goodwill toward the firm: Financial versus non-financial impacts. *Journal of Business Research*, 38(2), 141–159.

Newhagen, J., & Nass, C. (1989). Differential criteria for evaluating credibility of newspapers and TV news. *Journalism Quarterly*, 66(2), 277–289.

Newsom, D. V. (2001). *International public relations*. Thousand Oaks: Sage.

Nwagbara, U., & Reid, P. (2013). Corporate Social Responsibility (CSR) and Management Trends: Changing Times and Changing Strategies. *Economic Insights-Trends & Challenges*, 65(2), 12–19.

O'Connor, A., & Shumate, M. (2010). An economic industry and institutional level of analysis of corporate social responsibility communication. *Management Communication Quarterly*, 24(4), 529–551.

Oh, J., & Ki, E.-J. (2019). Factors affecting social presence and word-of-mouth in corporate social responsibility communication: Tone of voice, message framing, and online medium type. *Public Relations Review*, 45(2), 319–331.

Pérez, A., Del Mar García de los Salmones, M., & Tingchi Liu, M. (2019). Maximising business returns to corporate social responsibility communication: An empirical test. *Business Ethics: A European Review*, 28(3), 275–289.

Petty, R., & Cacioppo, J. (1986). *Communication and persuasion*. New York: Springer-Verlag.

Pirsch, J., Gupta, S., & Grau, S. (2007). A framework for understanding corporate social responsibility programs as a continuum: An exploratory study. *Journal of Business Ethics*, 70(2), 125–140.

Pivato, S, Misani, N., & Tencati, A. (2008). The impact of corporate social responsibility on consumer trust: The case of organic food. *Business Ethics: A European Review*, 17(1), 3–12.

Place, K. R. (2015). Exploring the role of ethics in public relations program evaluation. *Journal of Public Relations Research*, 27(2), 118.

Plowman, K. D., & Wilson, C. (2018). Strategy and tactics in strategic communication: Examining their intersection with social media use. *International Journal of Strategic Communication*, 12(2), 125–144.

Podnar, K. (2008). Communicating corporate social responsibility. *Journal of Marketing Communication*, 14(2), 75–81.

Pomering, A., & Johnson, L. (2009). Constructing a corporate social responsibility reputation using corporate image advertising. *Austalasian Marketing Journal*, 17, 106–114.

Porter, M., & Kramer, M. (2003). The competitive advantage of corporate philanthropy. In Harvard Business School, *Harvard Business Review on Corporate Social Responsibility* (pp. 27–64). Boston: Harvard Business School Publishing Corporation.

Public Relations Society of America (PRSA) (2022). About public relations. https://www.prsa.org/about/all-about-pr

Reilly, A. H., & Hynan, K. A. (2014). Corporate communication, sustainability, and social media: It's not easy (really) being green. *Business Horizons*, 57(6), 747–758.

Rockland, D. B. (2015). Comparing Barcelona Principles 1.0 and 2.0. *Public Relations Tactics*, 22(11), 7.

Rucker, D., & Petty, R. (2006). Increasing the effectiveness of communications to consumers: Recommendations based on elaboration likelihood and attitude certainty perspectives. *Journal of Public Policy and Marketing*, 25(1), 39–52.

Rybalko, S., & Seltzer, T. (2010). Dialogic communication in 140 characters or less: How Fortune 500 companies engage stakeholders using Twitter. *Public Relations Review*, 36(4), 336–341.

Saat, R. M., & Selamat, M. H. (2014). An examination of consumer's attitude towards corporate social responsibility (CSR) web communication using media richness theory. *Procedia-Social and Behavioral Sciences*, 155, 392–397.

Saxton, G. D., Gomez, L., Ngoh, Z., Lin, Y.-P., & Dietrich, S. (2019). Do CSR messages resonate? Examining public reactions to firms' CSR efforts on social media. *Journal of Business Ethics*, 155(2), 359.

Saxton, G. D., Ren, C., & Guo, C. (2021). Responding to diffused stakeholders on social media: Connective power and firm reactions to CSR-related Twitter messages. *Journal of Business Ethics*, 172(2), 229–252.

Schriner, M., Swenson, R., & Gilkerson, N. (2017). Outputs or outcomes? Assessing public relations evaluation practices in award-winning PR campaigns. *Public Relations Journal*, 11(1), ISSN 1942–4604.

Sen, S., & Bhattacharya, C. (2001). Does doing good always lead to doing better? Corporate reactions to corporate social responsibility. *Journal of Marketing*, 38(2), 225–243.

Servaes, H., & Tamayo, A. (2013). The impact of corporate social responsibility on firm value: The role of customer awareness. *Management Science*, 59(May), 1045–1061.

Signitzer, B., & Prexl, A. (2008). Corporate sustainability communications. *Journal of Public Relations Research*, 20(1), 1–19.

Singh, T., Veron-Jackson, L., & Cullinane, J. (2008). A new play in your marketing game plan. *Business Horizons*, 51(4), 281–292.

Skarmeas, D., & Leonidou, C. (2013). When consumers doubt, watch out! The role of CSR skepticism. *Journal of Business Research*, 66(10), 1831–1838.

Spangler, I., & Pompper, D. (2011). Corporate social responsibility and the oil industry: Theory and perspective fuel a longitudinal view. *Public Relations Review*, 37(3), 217–225.

Spanx Foundation (2022). The Red Backpack Fund. http://www.spanxfoundation.com/

Springston, J. (2001). Public relations and new media technology. In R. Heath, ed., *Handbook of public relations* (pp. 603–614). Thousand Oaks: Sage.

Starbucks (2022). Becoming resource positive. https://www.starbucks.com/responsibility/planet

Starck, K., & Kruckeberg, D. (2001). Public relations and community. In *Handbook of Public Relations* (pp. 51–60). Thousand Oaks: Sage.

Sternthal, B., Dholakia, R., & Leavitt, C. (1978). The persuasive effect of source credibility: Tests of cognitive response. *Journal of Consumer Research*, 4(4), 252–260.

Sundar, S. (1998). Effect of attribution on perception of online news stories. *Journalism and Mass Communication Quarterly*, 75(1), 55–68.

Sweetin, V., Knowles, L., Summey, J., & McQueen, K. (2013). Willingness-to-punish the corporate brand for corporate social irresponsibility. *Journal of Business Research*, 66(10), 1822–1830.

Sweetser, K. (2010). A losing strategy: The impact of nondisclosure in social media on relationships. *Journal of Public Relations*, 22(3), 288–312.

Szuba, P., & Tworzydło, D. (2020). Methods of measuring the effects of public relations activities applied by PR specialists in their professional work. *Marketing of Scientific and Research Organisations*, 35(1), 113–134.

Talkwalker (2021). Social media industry reports. https://www.talkwalker.com/social-media-industry-reports

Tan, S. H., Yeo, S. F., Goh, M. L., Chong, S. W., & Cheah, C. S. (2014). Factors that influence green purchase behaviour among young consumers. In *Advanced materials research*, vol. 1051 (pp. 1035–1039). Trans Tech Publications.

Thorson, K., Michaelson, D., Gee, E., Jian, J., Luan, G., Weatherly, K., Pung, S., Qin, Y., & Xu, J. (2015). Joining the movement? Investigating standardization of measurement and evaluation within public relations. *Research Journal of the Institute for Public Relations*, 2(1), 1–25.

Tian, Y., Hung, C., & Frumkin, P. (2020). An experimental test of the impact of corporate social responsibility on consumers' purchasing behavior: The mediation role of trust. *Corporate Social Responsibility and Environmental Management*, 27(6), 2972–2982.

Torres, A., Bijmolt, T., Tribo, J., & Verhoef, P. (2012). Generating global brand equity through corporate social responsibility to key stakeholders. *International Journal of Research in Marketing*, 29(1), 13–24.

Tylenol (2022). Supporting healthcare professionals. https://www.tylenol.com/cares

Upadhye, B. D., Das, G., & Varshneya, G. (2019). Corporate social responsibility: A boon or bane for innovative firms? *Journal of Strategic Marketing*, 27(1), 50–66.

Uzunoğlu, E., Türkel, S., & Akyar, B. Y. (2017). Engaging consumers through corporate social responsibility messages on social media: An experimental study. *Public Relations Review*, 43(5), 989–997.

Vallaster, C., Lindgreen, A., & Maon, F. (2012). Strategically leveraging corporate social responsibility: A corporate branding perspective. *California Management Review*, 54(3), 34–60.

Vlachos, P., Tsamakos, A., Vrechopoulos, A., & Avramidis, P. (2009). Corporate social responsibility: Attributions, loyalty and the mediating role of trust. *Journal of the Academy of Marketing Science*, 37(2), 170–180.

Vo, T. T., Xiao, X., & Ho, S. Y. (2019). How does corporate social responsibility engagement influence word of mouth on Twitter? Evidence from the airline industry. *Journal of Business Ethics*, 157(2), 525.

Wan, L., Poon, P., & Yu, C. (2013). Consumer reactions to corporate social responsibility brands: The role of face concern. *Journal of Consumer Marketing*, 33(1), 52–60.

Wang, A. (2011). Priming, framing and position on corporate social responsibility. *Journal of Public Relations Research*, 19(2), 123–145.

Wang, R., & Huang, Y. (2018). Communicating corporate social responsibility (CSR) on social media: How do message source and types of CSR messages influence stakeholders' perceptions? *Corporate Communications: An International Journal*, 23(3), 326–341.

Wang, Y., Cheng, Y., & Sun, J. (2021). When public relations meets social media: A systematic review of social media related public relations research from 2006 to 2020. *Public Relations Review*, 47(4), ISSN 0363-8111.

Watson, T. (2012). The evolution of public relations measurement and evaluation. *Public Relations Review*, 38(3), 390–398.

Wendy's (2020). Game on: Wendy's and Uber Eats team up to launch never stop gaming menu featuring five popular Twitch streamers. Retrieved https://www.prnewswire.com/news-releases/game-on-wendys-and-uber-eats-team-up-to-launch-never-stop-gaming-menu-

Werther, W., & Chandler, D. (2005). Strategic corporate social responsibility as global brand insurance. *Business Horizons*, 48(4), 317–324.

Westerwick, A. (2013). Effects of sponsorship, web site design, and Google ranking on the credibility of online information. *Journal of Computer-Mediated Communication*, 18(2), 194–211.

White, C., & Park, J. (2010). Public perceptions of public relations. *Public Relations Review*, 36(4), 319–324.

Worley, D. (2007). Relationship building in an Internet age. In S. Duhe, ed., *New Media and Public Relations* (pp. 145–157). New York: Peter Land Publishing.

Wright, D., & Hinson, M. (2009). An updated look at the impact of social media on public relations practice. *Public Relations Journal*, 3(2), 1–27.

Wright, D., & Hinson, M. (2010). An analysis of new communications media use in public relations: results of a five-year trend study. *Public Relations Journal*, 4(2), 1–27

Zaharia, C., & Zaharia, I. (2014). The greening of consumer culture. *Economics, Management & Financial Markets*, 9(1), 136–141.

Zerfass, A., Verčič, D., & Volk, S. (2017). Communication evaluation and measurement: Skills, practices and utilization in European organizations. *Corporate Communications: An International Journal*, 22(1), 2–18.

Zhang, J., & Swanson, D. (2006). Analysis of news media's representation of corporate social responsibility. *Public Relations Quarterly*, 51(2), 13–17.

Zyglidopoulos, S., Geogiadis, A., Carroll, C., & Siegel, D. (2011). Does media attention drive corporate social responsibility? *Journal of Business Research*, 65(11), 1622–1627.

Index

advertising, 23, 46, 49
advertising value equivalencies (AVEs), 30, 93
advocacy, 80–81
Afghanistan, 11
Airbnb, 12
AMEC, 90, 98
Amnesty International, 94
Argenti, 62
attribution, 24, 53
audience engagement, 48

Barcelona Principles of Measurement, 30, 43, 85, 88–90, 92, 97–98
brand, 9, 25, 60; attributes, 19; awareness, 24; equity, 20, 35; image, 24; loyalty, 54; reputation, 9; risks, 24; value, 19

Campbell's Soup, 11
carbon footprint, 20
Carroll, A., 7, 29, 76, 88, 99, 102
chief executive officer, 100; activism, 93
co-creation, 13, 15, 2, 24, 66, 76, 80, 81
cognitive processing, 40
communication loop, 62
communication planning, 27
communitarian (theory), 36, 39

content, 28, 49
control (message), 17, 34
convergence, 62
coronavirus, 24
corporate brand, 18; brand attributes, 19
corporate communication officer, 45
corporate identity, 50, 72
corporate image, 57
corporate reputation, 17, 20, 24, 26, 72
corporate social responsibility campaign, 48, 65, 74
Covid-19, 10, 14, 24, 48, 58
credibility, 48; information, 52, 65; news, 58; source, 65; tests, 59

dialogic communication, 14, 16, 36, 60–61, 64, 65, 100, 101
dialogue, 16
dominant coalition, 26, 38
Dove, 46, 53

eco-purchasing behavior, 71, 76
elaboration likelihood model, 13, 49
electronic word of mouth, 29, 37, 50, 58, 61, 64, 65, 82
ethics, 5, 70, 100
expert prescriber role, 7

Facebook, 51

fair trade, 73
feedback, 55
Fortune 500, 62
framing, 59
free flow of information, 37

global pandemic, 5, 12, 51, 53
goodwill, 6
green initiatives, 62
greenwashing, 17, 23, 53
Grunig, M., 16, 63; public relations models, 16, 63

Instagram, 51
Institute for Public Relations, 90
Intel, 10

key influencers, 91

Lyft, 11

marketing, 35; marketing communications efforts, 70
marketplace of ideas, 41
measurement, 31, 86, 97; frameworks, 90
media consumer, 65
media format, 9, 40, 48, 81; earned, 57; paid, 57; shared, 57; owned, 57
media relations, 28, 49, 59
message, 38
Microsoft, 10

negotiated brands, 13
news release, 28, 40

pandemic, 25, 33, 41, 47, 51
peripheral cues, 15
persuasion, 6
philanthropy, 6, 71, 78
press agent, 63
professional communicator, 24, 34
publicity agent, 8, 38
public relations professional, 7, 17, 26, 37–39, 47, 63, 67, 102, 103

publics, 48
purchase intent, 18, 26, 31, 54, 70, 74–75, 83
purchasing behavior, 73, 81

research, 9, 54
risk management, 19

self-promotion, 54
sensemaking, 28, 29, 47
shareholder, 29
skepticism, 15, 23, 31
social media, 12, 23, 24, 58, 73; measurement, 91–93
source, 35, 40, 60; credible, 50, 52; cues, 50; expertise, 58
Spanx, 94
special events, 28
spokesperson, 33; celebrity, 33
stakeholders, 5, 28, 53, 58, 67; communication, 83; groups, 19; involvement, 14, 34, 54; relationship, 73–74; trust, 75

tactician, 8
tactics, 28
Talkwalker, 93
thought leadership, 60
TikTok, 51, 96
transparency, 30, 37
trust, 42, 47; online, 52
trust factor, corporate social responsibility communication model, 26
Twitter, 62
two-step flow of communication, 34, 55
two-way symmetrical communication, 60, 63
Tylenol, 46

user-generated content, 45

viral communication, 59, 61
Virgin Group, 94

Wendy's, 94
word of mouth, 29, 57, 60, 66

YouTube, 96

About the Author

Kristie Byrum, Ph.D., APR, Fellow PRSA, is an international communications scholar with decades of rich experiences as a professor, business executive, and journalist, working in various roles in marketing, consulting, and entrepreneurism. She is an associate professor in the Media and Journalism Department at Bloomsburg University of Pennsylvania. Dr. Byrum teaches courses in public relations, media law, and media research. She has presented her scholarly work in the United States, Switzerland, Thailand, China, Norway, Canada, Greece, and Great Britain. She is a member of the Public Relations Society of America's prestigious College of Fellows. Dr. Byrum holds a doctorate in rhetorics, communication, and information design from Clemson University, a master of arts in journalism and mass communications from the University of South Carolina, and bachelor of arts in journalism from the Pennsylvania State University. She has written *The European Right to Be Forgotten: The First Amendment Enemy* (Lexington, 2018), served as co-author of *Strategic Communications Essentials*, and edited three books: *The Crisis Communications Reader, So You Want to Find a Job*, and *Public Relations Strategies and Tactics*. She has authored numerous scholarly articles and book chapters on public relations, ethics, and media law topics.

www.ingramcontent.com/pod-product-compliance
Lightning Source LLC
Chambersburg PA
CBHW021358300426
44114CB00012B/1274